COSPLAY FABRIC
FX

Painting, Dyeing & Weathering Costumes Like a Pro

Julianna Franchini

FanP◉weredPRESS
IMAGINE | MAKE | BECOME

Publisher: Amy Barrett-Daffin

Creative Director: Gailen Runge

Senior Editor: Roxane Cerda

Cover/Book Designer: April Mostek

Production Coordinator: Zinnia Heinzmann

Illustrator: Aliza Shalit

Photography Coordinator: Lauren Herberg

Photography Assistant: Gabriel Martinez

Front cover photography by John Rotor-Murphy

Photography by Juliana Franchini, unless otherwise noted

Page 11 (top): sirirak kaewgorn / Shutterstock.com

Page 11 (bottom): Gorloff-KV / Shutterstock.com

Page 16: Vineyard Perspective / Shutterstock.com

Page 40: plepann / Shutterstock.com

Page 46: P-fotography / Shutterstock.com

Page 53: Chaikom / Shutterstock.com

Page 54: Dmytro Buianskyi / Shutterstock.com

Page 93: Noel V. Baebler / Shutterstock.com

Published by FanPowered Press, an imprint of C&T Publishing, Inc., P.O. Box 1456, Lafayette, CA 94549

Attention Teachers: C&T Publishing, Inc., encourages the use of our books as texts for teaching. You can find lesson plans for many of our titles at ctpub.com or contact us at ctinfo@ctpub.com.

We take great care to ensure that the information included in our products is accurate and presented in good faith, but no warranty is provided, nor are results guaranteed. Having no control over the choices of materials or procedures used, neither the author nor C&T Publishing, Inc., shall have any liability to any person or entity with respect to any loss or damage caused directly or indirectly by the information contained in this book. For your convenience, we post an up-to-date listing of corrections on our website (ctpub.com). If a correction is not already noted, please contact our customer service department at ctinfo@ctpub.com or P.O. Box 1456, Lafayette, CA 94549.

Trademark (™) and registered trademark (®) names are used throughout this book. Rather than use the symbols with every occurrence of a trademark or registered trademark name, we are using the names only in the editorial fashion and to the benefit of the owner, with no intention of infringement.

Library of Congress Cataloging-in-Publication Data
Names: Franchini, Julianna, 1997- author.
Title: Cosplay fabric FX : painting, dyeing & weathering costumes like a
  pro / Julianna Franchini.
Other titles: Cosplay fabric effects
Description: Lafayette, CA : FanPowered Press, [2022] | Summary: "Learn key
  techniques and get detailed how-to instructions from a veteran cosplayer
  on special effects to enhance tiny details and give props and cosplays
  more dimension. Painting on fabric and weathering can transform cosplays
  from a simple costume to a garment that tells an entire story"--
  Provided by publisher.
Identifiers: LCCN 2022021410 | ISBN 9781644032374 (trade paperback) | ISBN
  9781644032381 (ebook)
Subjects: LCSH: Cosplay. | Costume. | Textile crafts.
Classification: LCC TT633 .F73 2022 | DDC 746/.0432--dc23/eng/20220613
LC record available at https://lccn.loc.gov/2022021410

Printed in the USA

10 9 8 7 6 5 4 3 2 1

Dedication

In memory of Fulvio and Jessie, who both introduced me to the joys of turning really weird materials into really cool stuff.

Acknowledgments

Firstly, I'd like to thank everyone at C&T Publishing for having faith in me and helping bring this book to life, especially my editor, Roxane Cerda, for guiding me through the process of writing my first book (it's a big task!) and Jessica for recommending me to the team in the first place. I also want to thank Christina for helping me make sure the safety sections in the book were up to par and Anthea Mallinson for not only helping me with safety as well but also introducing me to the incredibly deep world of dyeing and breakdown in the first place during my time at Capilano University. Thank you to my wonderful dad who shared his knowledge on airbrushes with me, as well as every cosplayer who has shared wisdom about paints and tools, helpful tips, and even common myths in the community. Finally, I want to thank my friends and family, who never stopped believing that I had it in me to research and write an entire book about how to make silly costumes.

COSPLAYER: Vic Trevino
COSTUME: Vicar Amelia from *Bloodborne*
Photo by David Ngo

CONTENTS

INTRODUCTION

Back when I was in school for costume design, one of my favourite classes was our dyeing and breakdown class, taught by Anthea Mallinson. Her enthusiasm for the subject was positively infectious. As early as the first day of the class, it became clear that every sweat stain, every pilled sweater texture, and every faded pocket and pant leg on a costume was painted, sanded, and dyed by hand by an artist. It was so mind blowing to find out how much thought went into both the big special effects that stole the show and the tiny details that made the characters feel human!

In the world of cosplay, where many resources are passed around on the internet, the art of costume weathering is, surprisingly, rarely talked about in depth. This is likely because it is so complex that it's kind of tricky to reduce into a single blog post or a snappy video tutorial. There are attempts, of course, but if you don't have professional training, it's difficult to tell which methods are legitimate and which are dubious. As a result, while many hobbyist cosplayers have been able to reach or even surpass the skill levels of entertainment-industry costumers when it comes to sewing and armour building, fabric weathering has never quite seen the same amount of fanfare and exploration from the community—which is nuts because there is clearly so much potential for geeking out hiding under the surface!

So, with the power of my formal education and my love of cosplay, I decided that I wanted to write a comprehensive, accessible guide to weathering and dyeing for cosplayers, as opposed to theatre and TV wardrobe teams, who have their own sets of needs. This turned out to be way more difficult than I thought. After months of working tirelessly with my editor to create something that made sense to an average Joe cosplayer and flowed reasonably well, I think we've finally done it!

I truly hope that this book will inspire you with the vast possibilities offered by painting and weathering fabrics. After all, what you can do with some sandpaper and acrylic paint will blow your mind.

COSPLAYER: Marquise Cubey
COSTUME: Gina Lestrade from *The Great Ace Attorney*
Photo by John Rotor-Murphy

COSPLAYER: Marquise Cubey
COSTUME: Protagonist from *Persona 3*
Photo by John Rotor-Murphy

PART 1

THE ART OF PLANNING

Fictional Danger, REAL SAFETY

While doing research for this book, I referred back to a lot of the dyeing and breakdown texts I used when I was learning costuming in college. Every one of them had something in common: an entire giant chapter about safety.

I also did research by talking to many of my cosplay peers in order to find out what sort of information cosplayers were interested in learning. Every one of them also had something much more worrying in common: a safety horror story!

While there is far more emphasis on safety in the cosplay community now than there used to be, sometimes information can still slip through the cracks, so even if a tutorial from the internet has lots of views and is made by a cosplayer you admire, it still doesn't automatically make it safe.

Since I have an entire book, it turns out that I actually get the rare opportunity to go into more detail about safety than a blog post or a video normally can. That being said, there's no way that this, or any, book could ever tell you how to protect yourself from every single potentially hazardous activity, so it's important to always read the specific safety information in the instructions of each material or tool you use.

COSPLAYER: Alexandra Hudson
COSTUME: Original Character inspired by the Star Wars franchise
Photo by David Ngo

Choosing a Safe Workspace

In order to protect yourself and the people and pets around you, many safety instructions will tell you to use the material in a ventilated space. Simply cracking open a window isn't going to cut it in most cases. So, what are your options?

Outdoors

While you still need to wear the personal protective equipment (PPE) required for the activities you are doing, working outdoors on a balcony or in a backyard is generally safe. The only drawback to working outdoors is, of course, the weather, especially since the humidity level and the temperature can affect paint drying.

Garages

If you're fortunate enough to have access to a house with a garage, use it! Garages have all of the benefits of working outdoors, plus they're sheltered from the elements and are an environment that you likely won't mind making a bit of a mess in.

Indoors with a Fan

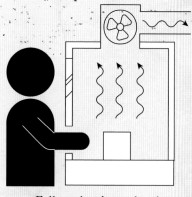

Fully enclosed spray booth

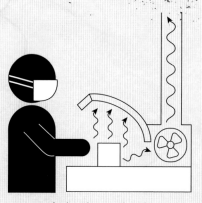

Airbrush spray booth

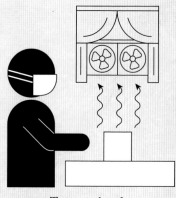

Twin window fan

Working inside your house isn't always ideal, but if you have no choice, you can still do certain things indoors. The best kind of ventilation fan to use indoors is a fully enclosed spray booth. It keeps all of the fumes inside the space, with the only holes being at the bottom for your hands. However, spray booths are big, permanent fixtures and while they can be built to almost any size you need with inexpensive hardware-store materials, they're not right for every crafter.

Fortunately, a partially enclosed airbrush spray booth is a more accessible alternative. They are smaller in size, but they are great for containing the fumes from adhesives and paints on smaller pieces.

The bare minimum you will need to ventilate a room is a built-in HVAC fan such as a bathroom fan or a twin window fan. These are a fairly accessible form of ventilation and are great to have turned on next to you when you are dying. However, the fumes are still floating around the room, so anyone in the room will need to wear a mask or respirator if the safety instructions require it.

HVAC FANS IN SHARED BUILDINGS

If you are using an HVAC fan in a bathroom for ventilation and you live in an apartment, you can help prevent fumes from reaching your neighbours (and the atmosphere) by replacing the filter in the fan beforehand. An activated carbon filter will keep harmful fumes and vapours at bay.

Protecting the Outside of Your Body

Your hands and your eyes are the parts of your body that you consciously use the most when crafting, so in order to keep using them to make cool things for a long time, it's vital to protect them from various hazards as you work.

Disposable Gloves

Basic medical gloves are available in latex and non-latex versions, and they're great for working with room temperature liquids such as paint and adhesives. Gloves are also just nice to have so that you can take them off and touch things like doorknobs and electronics without making a mess.

Leather Work Gloves

Sturdy gloves make it much easier and faster to sand and do other physical weathering without your hands getting scratched and scraped. Even when you're wearing gloves, remember to always cut away from your body.

Chemical-Resistant Rubber Gloves

These gloves are important for working with dyes. Long double-thickness gloves in particular are handy to insulate your skin from heat so that you can get your hands right into a hot dye bath if necessary.

Safety Goggles

Proper safety goggles provide more coverage than glasses, protecting your eyes more effectively on the sides, top, and bottom from dust and splashes.

Apron and Old Painting Clothes

An apron, old clothes, and even old shoes are just handy to wear when you're doing messy work.

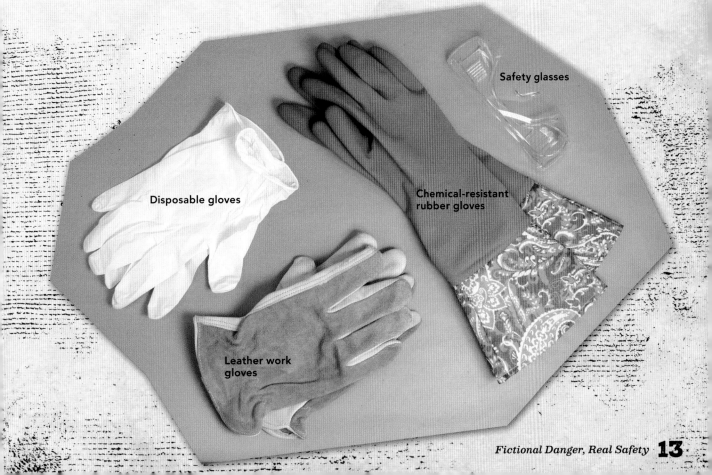

Safety glasses

Disposable gloves

Chemical-resistant rubber gloves

Leather work gloves

Protecting Your Lungs

Your lungs have the very important job of keeping you alive, and as you can probably guess, they're a lot less sturdy than your skin. Both chemical vapours and particles from sanding can not only make you feel sick, but they can also cause deadly illnesses from continued exposure, including silicosis and lung cancer. Keeping them out of your lungs is crucial!

Medical Masks

Normal surgical masks are an inexpensive way to protect your airways from dust particles that may float around when sanding, but they can't protect you from everything, especially much smaller particles or vapours. For even more protection against small particles, N95 masks approved by NIOSH (the National Institute for Occupational Safety and Health) are the most effective.

A cartridge respirator and medical masks

Cartridge Respirators

While the medical masks are great for dust and particles, they will not protect you from vapours. For these, you may need to wear a NIOSH-approved cartridge respirator, a cool-looking mask with detachable cartridge filters that can be switched out to protect your lungs from different substances, including dust. They are arguably the most important piece of protective equipment for building cosplays with more advanced materials, and as such, they are a slightly bigger investment than other pieces of PPE.

Your respirator mask should be secure enough that it won't fall off when you move your head, but not so tight that it gives you a headache. A quick-and-easy way to test your respirator's fit and seal can be done while wearing it.

With the filters off, put your hands over the holes where the filters normally screw in.

Cover these holes and inhale. The mask should collapse in on itself and not allow any air in.

If the test is successful and you can't inhale any air, the mask fits. If you can inhale air while covering the holes, adjust the straps and repeat the test until it is successful. If you cannot get the mask to work properly, purchase another mask and repeat the test.

RESPIRATOR MAINTENANCE

Respirator cartridges are good for approximately 36 continuous hours in open air. However, you can help your filters last much longer if you store them in an airtight, resealable ziplock bag when they're not in use. When you take them out and expose them to air, use a permanent marker to keep a tally of every hour you've used them. Once your tally reaches 36, it's time to toss them out and get new ones.

Finally, to keep germs at bay, make sure to clean out the inside of your mask each time you use it with a non-alcohol-based wipe.

If all of this seems daunting or if you aren't able to wear a respirator for some reason, the great news is that not every technique requires one, and you can still get incredibly far in the world of cosplay without one. Playing around with safer materials and techniques to see if you can achieve a similar outcome can be just as fun and rewarding, and if that fails, you can always bribe a friend with a nice lunch to help you out with the parts of your cosplay that cannot be done without a respirator.

RESPIRATOR FIT TESTS

If you're planning on investing in a half-mask respirator and it's your first time purchasing one, see if you can find an authorized facility in your area where you can book a professional in-person fit test. This is the best and most reliable way to ensure that your respirator will fit and seal properly. After all, there's not much worse than spending money on a respirator that doesn't work because it's the wrong size!

If you are required to wear a mask to work, it is also recommended (and required by many government workplace safety associations) that you have your respirator professionally fit or refit every one to two years or immediately following any cosmetic or dental surgery that alters the shape of your nose or jaw.

Using Products and Materials Safely

Reading the safety instructions on the manufacturer's packaging is vital to using any product safely; however, the package instructions can sometimes be limited. A small package may not be large enough to convey every single thing you need to know, and package instructions only account for using the product the "proper" way.

If you plan to use a product as intended, you are likely okay to go ahead after reading the regular package instructions. However, this isn't always the case with cosplay and especially weathering, where many popular techniques are instead built on pushing a material to its limits. For example, what if you need to expose a common material to extreme heat to shape it or get a cool-looking effect? How would you know whether it's safe and how to protect yourself?

The great news is that even more detailed safety information is just a quick internet search away, all contained in a document called a material safety data sheet, or MSDS for short.

An MSDS exists for nearly every non-fabric cosplay-making material, from adhesives and dyes to spray paint and even EVA foam. If you do an internet search with your material's name followed by "MSDS," you should be able to find a downloadable version of the sheet that you can read, or at the very least, an official email address or website where it is available upon request.

SAFETY FIRST!

Every time you learn a cool new technique from this book or another cosplay tutorial, look up the safety information and the MSDS for any materials that are required before you purchase them. This is especially important if you're on a budget or live in an apartment where proper ventilation is hard to achieve.

Reading a Material Safety Data Sheet: A Guide for Non-Chemistry Nerds

Safety data sheets can be long and, let's be real, chances are we aren't doing anything industrial that requires us to know absolutely everything about a material. So, here are the sections that I have found the most useful for cosplayers and costume makers. An MSDS may change the wording of the section titles slightly, but the section numbers always stay the same.

SECTION 2: HAZARDS IDENTIFICATION

This section has the full list of the material's potential hazards if there are any. Keep in mind that it still only includes hazards from using the product as intended, and it won't cover potential hazards from using tools or other products with it.

SECTION 4: EMERGENCY AND FIRST AID PROCEDURES

In the unlikely event that you become injured or sick and you have reason to believe it's due to chemical exposure, bring the MSDS with you to the doctor so that they will know exactly how to help.

SECTION 5: FIREFIGHTING MEASURES

If you plan to use the material near heat or flame, familiarize yourself with the extinguishing media section. Most fires can be put out with water or regular fire extinguishers; however, pouring water on some types of fires (such as grease fires) will make them worse.

SECTION 6: ACCIDENTAL RELEASE MEASURES

If you spill the material, this section will list any other materials or cleaners that may react badly with it (bleach and ammonia, for example, is a deadly combination).

SECTION 8: EXPOSURE CONTROL AND PERSONAL PROTECTION

This is where you can find the exact PPE you will need in order to work with the material.

SECTION 10: STABILITY AND REACTIVITY

In cosplay, using materials for unintended purposes is part of the fun. Decomposition products are the key thing to look out for in this section, particularly for materials you plan to use heat on. Some thermoplastics such as Worbla's Finest Art are designed to be stable and safe at high temperatures, but most plastics, including EVA foam and puffy fabric paint, may start to chemically break down when heated and produce toxic vapours or gases.

SAFETY FIRST!

If you are heating up a material that produces toxic vapours at high temperatures, you must do so in a place with very good ventilation and wear a respirator with cartridges meant for organic vapours, even if it doesn't say so on the MSDS.

SECTION 13: DISPOSAL CONSIDERATIONS

If you're considering washing or dumping this stuff down the sink, this section will tell you whether or not that's a good idea.

LIKE A PRO

Unlike sewing an original costume, when you're trying to imitate a garment that was designed and made by another person, *weathering* is the act of replicating something a lot more nebulous: the physical history of a garment. It can be tough to know where to start!

The way I was taught to approach this process was to begin by putting myself into the character's shoes. As we broke down designs to make them into real costumes, we got into the habit of asking the most minute, personal questions about the character's life. If the writer or director didn't have an answer, we'd fill in the gaps ourselves. These details could range from physical events, such as the cause of a hole in their sleeve, all the way to borderline-invasive character tidbits, like how long it has been since they last took a shower.

And then, one day, it hit me. I'd done all this before. It's just that when I did it, it was called writing fanfiction.

COSPLAYER: Marquise Cubey
COSTUME: Little Sister from *Bioshock 2*
Photo by John Rotor-Murphy

Starting with the Story and Headcanon

If you're deep enough in any fandom subcultures, you're likely familiar with the term *headcanon*, which describes a fan's read-between-the-lines interpretations of characters and events that transpired offscreen or outside a piece of media. Nearly every form of transformative fan art and fanfiction draws from the creator's headcanon, and yes, this includes cosplay! Even if you happen to be blessed with perfect references, weathering can be different from many other cosplay disciplines because the story and your headcanon can affect the approach you take just as much as the way something looks.

COSTUME: Rey from *Star Wars: The Force Awakens*
Photo by Jennifer Renzy

Being Practical

Much like any other part of cosplaying, you may not have the time, budget, or facilities to do everything you want to do. Fortunately, since the world of weathering is so vast, there are just as many expensive and time-consuming methods to achieve a certain look as there are cheap and quick ones.

Finally, one of the most important things that separates the good costume makers from the great is the physical stability of their garments. This is especially important when you are tearing up your garment, so it may not hurt to cheat and hand sew the occasional torn piece of fabric into place here and there to prevent wardrobe malfunctions.

Questions to Ask About a Character's Story Before Weathering

Before we jump into the process of weathering a costume, it helps to really familiarize yourself not just with a character's visual design, but also their story, as you will be replicating these aspects in your weathering.

- How old is the character's outfit? Is it brand new or faded and stained?

- Does the character take good care of their stuff and take pride in how they look, only care that their clothing is functional, or care so little about their clothing that it is broken down and no longer functional?

- What kind of environment has the character been hanging out in? Is it dry or damp? What colour is the soil? How long have they been there?

- Has the character been wearing the outfit outside? Would parts of it, such as the hood and shoulders, have been rained on?

COSTUME: Tess from *The Last of Us*
Photo by Jennifer Renzy

Even though you can only see the back of the shoulder in this photograph, you can already learn a ton about this character's life just based on the weathering, from the broken-down backpack to tiny details like the stain on her sleeve suggesting a previous bloody nose.

- Does the character have a messy occupation?

- Has the character been in a battle or a fight? What weapons would have been used? What sort of fighter is the character? Are they reckless, meaning they might have more battle damage?

Obviously, you are under no obligation to know or even care about the answers to any of these questions, but when you think about the small details, odds are you just might get a great idea that you wouldn't have otherwise! For instance, you may already know that Kylo Ren wears a tattered cape, but what if the holes had a touch of grey ash around the edges in reference to him being careless with his lightsaber? What if your sweater for Freddy Kreuger was not just dirty and ripped, but also covered in dull, dried bloodstains on the sleeves near his hands?

Questions to Ask About Scope Before Weathering

Now that you know the most important parts of the story that you want to tell, you need to figure out how your approach may change depending on your practical situation.

- Which effects will be the most noticeable and should be prioritized?

- What is my budget?

- How much time do I have to make this costume?

- Do I have access to the proper ventilation and protective equipment to safely do everything I want?

- Is this costume for a contest, or am I just having fun with special effects for my own personal satisfaction?

- Are there pieces such as socks or a petticoat that may not be visible all the time, but could potentially show? Do I need to dye or weather them as well so they don't throw off the look?

- Are there pieces I don't want to ruin permanently with paint or rips? Do I need to weather them with temporary techniques?

Keeping both your story and your scope in mind from the very start will do wonders to help you plan out your cosplay and get even more out of the time and tools you have.

Now that you have a vision for the look and backstory of your character and an understanding of your available resources, you can dive into planning out the specific decisions that will get you there.

Picking the Perfect
COLOURS

If I wanted to draw a picture of Naruto on my computer right now, I could very easily find an online image and use the eyedropper tool in my program of choice to grab the exact #f7954e orange to colour in his jacket. However, if I wanted to make a cosplay of Naruto, I can't just look for, or even dye, my own precise #f7954e orange fabric—that would be silly.

Fortunately, even when there may be dozens of orange fabrics in the world to choose from, we can use colour theory to make informed decisions and choose fabrics that look fantastic together. The great thing about colour is that it's completely relative and as long as every colour in your costume meshes, you'll look amazing no matter what!

(Warning: This is the chapter where my Canadianness becomes incredibly apparent.)

COSPLAYER: Redfield
COSTUME: Poison Ivy original design inspired by DC Comics
Photo by Masahiro_ Tsumi

The Colour Wheel (A Very Basic Refresher to Start Us Off)

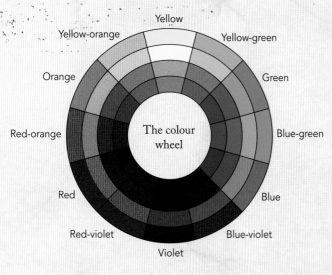

When we are working with colour, it helps to be familiar with five types of colours on the colour wheel.

PRIMARY COLOURS, for our purposes, are red, yellow, and blue. We can mix these together to get all kinds of colours.

SECONDARY COLOURS are orange, green, and purple, and they are achieved by mixing two primary colours.

TERTIARY COLOURS are primary colours mixed with secondary colours. These include vermillion (red and orange), turquoise (blue and green), and chartreuse (yellow and green), to name a few.

ANALOGOUS COLOURS are right next to each other on the colour wheel. Use analogous colours when you want something to look unified.

COMPLEMENTARY COLOURS are on opposite sides of the colour wheel. Use complementary colours when you want things to pop and stand out.

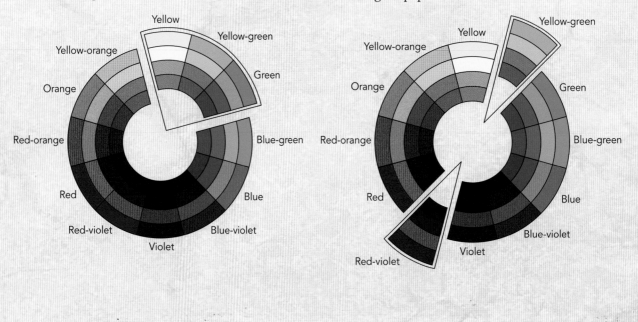

Temperature

The closer a colour is to orange on the colour wheel, the warmer it is. Colours that are closer to blue on the colour wheel are considered cooler.

This may sound obvious to some folks; after all, most of us were taught that orange, red, and yellow are warm colours and blue, purple, and green are cool. Like many things in nature, though, colour *temperature* is a spectrum, not binary, and this way of thinking helps us tell the difference between a warmer and cooler version of the same colour.

As an exercise, refer to the colour wheel diagram on the previous page and see if you can tell which row of the same basic colours is the cooler one, and which is warmer:

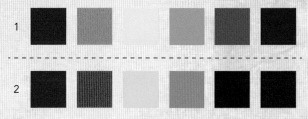

Answer: The colours in row 1 are warmer, and those in row 2 are cooler.

Saturation

The *saturation* of a colour refers to how bright or dull the colour is. When it comes to pigments, mixing two complementary colours with each other will make the colour duller and less intense. As you can see, it also has the double effect of nudging the colour temperature in a more neutral direction as well.

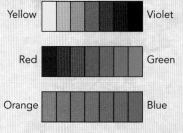

Practical Colour Theory in Cosplay

The most effective way to choose paint and fabric colours for a cosplay is to start with the thing that is the hardest to change the colour of and choose your colours based around that. This could be anything from a piece that you've borrowed to multiple garments you simply do not have the time to dye. Most notably, unless you're cosplaying as something like a green space alien, your skin colour can't be changed.

Sometimes, you may have your heart set on a character but, tragically, they wear a colour that you don't find particularly flattering, such as bright red, lemon yellow, or Naruto's #f7954e orange. In this case, a good trick is to go through your own closet, pick out your favourite clothes, and see if there are any common colour themes—namely, whether they tend to be warmer, cooler, brighter, or duller. Then, when you pick out costume colours, see if you can find or dye your fabric to a shade that's slightly warmer or cooler (based on the theme you found) than the original desired colour.

Artistic Colour Theory in Cosplay

To take things a step further, colour temperature is also often used to show character traits, and it's something that may help you decide between similar shades of fabric, dye, and paint colours that you're considering for your cosplay.

Generally, an overall warmer palette is good for characters who are friendly, heroic, or just plain adorable. It can also read as antique or connected to nature.

A subtly cooler palette is great for antiheroes, rebels, and lonely characters. Cool colours also generally read as futuristic or magical.

WHITES AND OFF-WHITES

Pure white fabric is often very hard to photograph and balance. If you plan on photographing your cosplay, instead of a pure, bright white, try using an off-white (warmer) or very light grey (cooler) fabric depending on what you want your overall colour temperature to be.

Weathering Colours

As soon as you begin to weather a costume, you are going to be thinking about the colour of dirt a lot more than you're used to!

These are some common colours that are used in the entertainment industry to imply different types of weathering, and some subtle colour temperature distinctions can end up being more noticeable than you'd think.

Clean Shadows

For seam shading that isn't necessarily meant to read as dirt or staining, use paint that matches the colour of the original fabric as closely as you can find, and mix it with a hint of a cooler black, such as carbon black.

Brown Dirt

Raw umber is a cool, greenish-brown, and burnt umber is a warmer, reddish-brown. These two colours can also be mixed if you'd prefer something more neutral. If you are using these to paint dirt and they're darker than you want them to be, or if you just want to create some layering and highlights, mix them with some buff titanium, a creamy off-white sometimes also called raw titanium.

Paint used to suggest a sandy environment

Photo by Alexandra Hudson

Sand

Raw sienna is a light, slightly orange beige, and it's the perfect colour to mimic desert sand. It can also be mixed or layered with buff (or raw) titanium for highlights and with burnt sienna for a rich, dark reddish-orange.

Grass and Plant Stains

Warm, dull, yellowish greens such as chromium oxide green are great to use on their own or mixed in with other colours for organic-looking grass stains and ocean grime.

The Forbidden, Nasty Colours

If you're wondering where to find scarier weathering colours for things like blood and mould, look in Extreme Weathering and Fake Blood (page 116) where you can also find the rest of the more detailed horror FX.

This paint reads as plant stains

Photo by Redfield

The Layered Process of
WEATHERING

Weathering is like a delicious cake, or perhaps an onion if you prefer that comparison: It has layers! The order in which you do your weathering is extremely important to both the look and the story, especially when you're making a heavily weathered cosplay with multiple colours and effects.

The most practical reason for layered weathering is that certain steps such as dyeing are simply easier to do on a garment that isn't caked in paint, so they are usually done first. Additionally, tearing up and fading a costume can also cause paint and dye to rub off, revealing the cleaner, unpainted threads underneath. Unless you have a good story reason for this, it may not be what you want. Most importantly, if you're painting a big dramatic splatter or burn mark onto a costume, you likely won't want your big focal point to be obscured by layers of dirt; that's why the biggest effects are usually saved for last.

A MORE PRACTICAL PROCESS

You don't have to do all of these steps in the exact order outlined in this chapter; they're merely guidelines to help you out. If, for instance, doing all of your physical weathering at once and then doing all of the painting makes more sense to you, then you should absolutely do that! You should continue working in layers within those steps, however, such as doing your physical aging first and your physical battle damage last.

COSPLAYER: Lutavia Cosplay
COSTUME: San from *Princess Mononoke*
Photo by Jonathan Vilches

Layer 1: Colouring, Staining, and Ageing

Because a garment's age affects its very foundation on a molecular level, these effects are ones that you almost always want to add to your costume first.

Fabric and Base

If you're making your costume from scratch and you plan to weather your costume fairly heavily, there are some tricks and considerations to keep in mind. Check out Building Costumes to Be Destroyed (page 74) before you get stitching.

Dyeing

Dyeing is often a critical step in making sure that you have the exact base colour you envisioned, making an existing garment or fabric appear older, or adding fake stains or visual texture.

To achieve a custom colour, check out Dyeing Solid Colours (page 62). A common way to show that something is old is by dyeing it a duller colour. Using a very subtle shade of brown or grey is a popular method, but the most effective way to approach weathering is to dye it with its complementary colour. For instance, if you're ageing a blue shirt, dyeing it with black tea will actually add a bit of orange to it and dull the colour; a bright red would be best toned down by dyeing it slightly green.

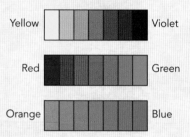

To determine the best overdyeing colour for ageing, select a light complementary colour of the base colour.

Dye can also be used in selective places to create gradients, stains, texture, and patterns. Once you've learned about dyeing solid colours, check out Creating Patterns and Texture with Dye (page 66) for even more dye ideas.

COSPLAYER: Marquise Cubey
COSTUME: Lup Taako Original Design
inspired by *The Adventure Zone*
Photo by Lorna Phillips

Layer 2: Wear from Being Worn

If you've ever examined your own well-loved jeans and shoes in your closet, you may be quite familiar with the next level of costume weathering, which focuses on how a garment breaks down with continued use.

Fading and Physical Wear

For clothing to look lived in, it should be faded in key places, and this can be done with any number of sandpaper techniques as described in Texture and Fading (page 77). These key places include joints like knees and elbows, but also any other high-traffic areas such as hems and pockets.

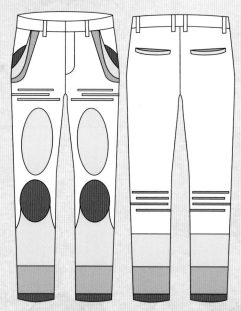

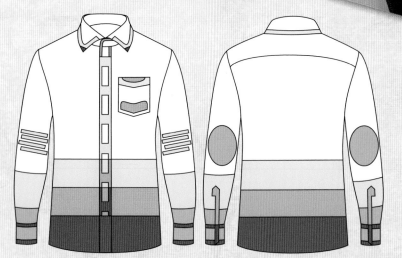

Key weathering zones on a button-down shirt. Red zones are generally the most heavily weathered, orange areas have medium weathering, and yellow areas are lightly weathered.

Key weathering zones on a pair of pants

Holes and Repairs

If you want the holes in your garment to read as being from wear, they should be large and soft. To get softer margins on your holes you can use either the sandpaper and rock techniques to create soft holes in these key areas, or you can cut the holes with a blade and then manually pull at the threads for more control over the shape and size. For a full rundown of sandpaper and rock techniques, check out Holes, Cuts, and Rips (page 88).

A way to imply that there is a hole in a garment without actually cutting into it is to sew a repair, such as a patch, over an imaginary hole. Check out Visible Repairs (page 81) for ideas.

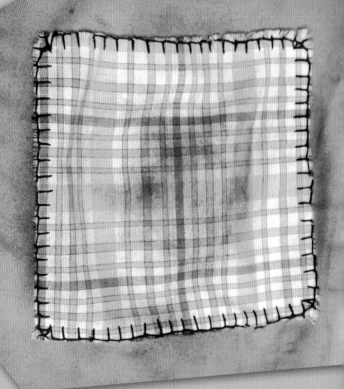

Layer 3: Shadows and Dirt

This is probably the most versatile type of weathering, and it's your secret weapon if you want any costume to look straight out of a Hollywood movie.

Soaked-In Stains and Colour

When you want to achieve the look of a watery, soaked-in stain such as spilled coffee, blood, mud, seawater, and the like, these sorts of stains should be the first thing you paint on so they sit underneath surface stains.

Larger stained areas can be created with dyes so that your fabric remains soft; see The Right Dye for Your Project (page 43) to be sure you select the best dye for the look you want to achieve with the technique you plan to use. Check out Creating Patterns and Texture with Dye (page 66) for techniques to add those stains.

Smaller stains can be created with watered-down paint. To get the full scoop on how to create these, refer to Wet Stains and Splatters (page 112). Gradient dyeing along hems can add stained effects to the margins of a garment; see Dip-Dyeing (page 69).

Dry Brushing and Shading

The same dry brushing techniques that work great for shadows are also perfect for adding dry dirt and dust to key areas; see Realistic Shading and Dirt (page 108).

Even if you're a sewing-focused cosplayer who is hesitant to paint the beautiful outfits that you worked so hard to make, painting in shadows can actually help make even the flattest and hardest to photograph fabrics stand out, helping to accentuate your hard work.

Layer 4: Battle Damage and Event-Based Weathering

This is where the big dramatic stuff happens! Since you want this layer to really steal the show, it'll be the last thing you do so that it can sit on top of all the layers you have been building up.

Tears and Slashes

Tears and slashes can help your costume tell a story. Different shapes and ways of creating them can be used to imply different causes, such as blades or regular wear and tear, and you can find out how to create these in Holes, Cuts, and Rips (page 88).

Decomposition

This category includes creating effects ranging from burns and ash to gross zombie stains, which are outlined in Extreme Weathering and Fake Blood (page 116). These are also some of the last effects to add to your costume so they stand out rather than recede into the background.

Fresh Splatters and Dirt

When you are telling a story with a costume, the most recent effects are the last ones you'll add. These can be anything from a big oil splatter on a mechanic's coveralls to a mud stain on a coat to a bright red spaghetti sauce spill on the apron of an evil chef. Since these effects are usually big, they will often be done with fabric paint, fabric ink, or watered-down paint so that the fabric doesn't get stiff. Check these out in Wet Stains and Splatters (page 112).

COSPLAYER: CocoaSugarCosplay

COSTUME: Anthy from original fan art by Dessi_Desu, inspired by *Revolutionary Girl Utena*

Photo by Felix Dandy

PART 2

THE SCIENCE OF DYEING

What Is DYE?

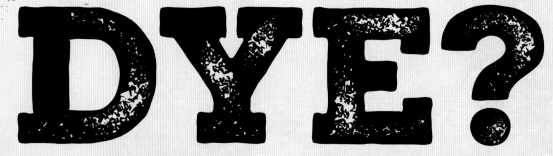

Paint suspends pigment in a medium such as acrylic or oil that sits on top of an object when you apply it, but dye is a special pigment that, when dissolved in water, creates a solution that bonds chemically with the fibre you're dyeing, turning it a different colour.

When you dye something, as opposed to painting it, the added colour is translucent and practically weightless, meaning that you're able to preserve the quality of the texture underneath, whether it's a patterned fabric, a wig, or even a transparent hard object such as a resin gemstone.

Due to its transparent nature, you can only dye something a darker colour than it was before, so you will need to keep in mind that the original colour will be mixed in. This means that while you may not be able to dye a bright red shirt perfectly blue, you can make it purple, brown, or some other colour with a lot of red in it.

COSPLAYER: Marquise Cubey
COSTUME: Little Sister from *Bioshock 2*
Photo by John Rotor-Murphy

What Is Dye Used For?

Dyeing is very often used as a problem-solving technique, giving you the ability to tweak or change the colour of wigs and fabric. Dye can be used for anything from toning down an unflattering shade to refreshing an old wig to suit a new character to even changing a fabric that traditionally comes in only boring colours to the brighter one you need for that cartoon character.

Dyeing is also a fun, cool, and creative technique for weathering. Dyeing is super useful in this context to create large, dark, saturated stains while keeping the original texture and drape of the fabric intact and to add visual age to a garment. Subtle dye baths are awesome for toning down colours to add age, and you can even add overall visual texture by using various resist techniques, see Resist Dyeing (page 66).

Of course, fabric dyeing can also be used to make your own custom textiles. This can mean anything from dyeing sections of your fabric different colours to intentionally painting, crumpling, or tying resists into your fabric to create patterns during dyeing.

COSPLAYER: Marquise Cubey
COSTUME: Gina Lestrade from *The Great Ace Attorney*
Photo by John Rotor-Murphy

COSPLAYER: Redfield
COSTUME: Poison Ivy original design inspired by DC Comics
Photo by Masahiro_ Tsumi

FIBRE CONTENT

Unlike painting, dyeing is a chemical process, so naturally, there are certain dyes that work on certain types of fibres better than others. The term *fibre* refers to the substance your material—whatever it is you're dyeing—is made of. You're likely even more familiar with the concept of fibres than you think; one of the most common places they appear is that "80% cotton, 20% polyester" tag on your shirt.

Fibre is not to be confused with the weave of a fabric. For instance, satin is a type of weave that refers to a soft, shiny fabric used for special occasions. However, satin can be made out of many different types of fibres, such as silk, polyester, or rayon. Those three materials—while they may look and feel similar at first glance—are all made out of completely different fibres, with different molecules that will all dye very differently.

Types of Fibres

For our purposes, there are three different types of dyeable fibres that you will come across: cellulose, protein, and synthetic.

Not all fibres are created equal, even ones that are the same type, and some like to soak up colour more easily than others. To show this in action, the fibres that you can see in the photos on the next page were all dyed with the same dyes at the same concentration. Keep this in mind when you're thinking about what fabric to use.

Cellulose Fibres

These fibres are made from various plants. Here are a few that you may have heard of, including man-made fibres with a cellulose base. These were dyed with Rit All-Purpose Dye in Royal Blue at 2% concentration.

From left to right: cotton, linen, rayon viscose (made from wood pulp, often bamboo), and lyocell (sometimes sold under the brand name Tencel)

From left to right: wool (sheep), silk, genuine leather, fur (alpaca), nylon, and nylon mesh (leather and fur samples were recycled from responsibly sourced offcuts)

Protein Fibres

This type includes virtually all animal products and yes, silkworms are part of the animal kingdom. These samples were dyed with Rit All-Purpose Dye in Wine at 2% concentration. Nylon is a synthetic fibre, but it is unique in that it also takes dyes meant for protein fibres, so it is included in this category and in Synthetic Fibres (below).

SAFETY FIRST!

Technically, human hair is also a protein, and while the dyes mentioned in this book may work on a human hair wig or hair extensions, keep these chemicals far away from the hair growing on your head!

Synthetic Fibres

Synthetics are one of the most common fibres you will come across in cosplay. All of these are man-made with a variety of different bases and processes. These were dyed with Rit DyeMore Synthetic Dye in Graphite at 2% concentration

From left to right: polyester, acrylic, polyester/spandex blend, nylon, nylon mesh, vinyl (opaque), vinyl (clear), and synthetic wig fibre

NOT JUST FOR FABRIC

Dyeing doesn't just stop at soft things. If you have a gemstone or some other transparent object made from almost any plastic, it can be dyed with disperse dyes meant for synthetic fabrics, which may sometimes be easier than painting it.

IDENTIFYING MYSTERY FIBRES ... WITH SCIENCE!

EXPERIMENT FIRST

Try burning some scrap fabrics that you fully know the fibre content of before testing any mystery fabrics. This will help you know what to look for, especially if you think the mystery fabric may be a blend of two different fibres.

SAFETY FIRST!

Conduct your burn test away from anything flammable or explosive, including wood, curtains, long sleeves and hair, paper, carpet, and aerosol cans.

Sometimes, you might find a fabric that you want to dye in your stash, a thrift store, or a clearance bin, only to be filled with dread when you see the "100% unknown fibres" tag, or no tag at all. If you've been around enough fabrics, you may be able to tell the approximate fibre contents based on the drape and feel; however, your intuition may not always be able to tell you if that a fabric is a blend. Fortunately, there's a very sophisticated and scientific way to tell different fibres apart: setting them on fire. (Yes, seriously!)

Much like how different fibres react in unique ways to different dyes, they also react in unique ways to something else far faster and easier to test: fire! The quickest way to determine the approximate fibre contents of a mystery fabric is to burn a teeny-tiny swatch. Here's how you can do your own burn tests at home.

SAFETY FIRST!

If your fibre is burning more rapidly than you expected and you start to feel even slightly uncomfortable, simply drop it onto the tinfoil and let it burn out. Never shake anything that's on fire!

Process

1. Cover the baking pan with tinfoil. Place the unlit candle in the centre of the pan. Set the container of water nearby where it's easy to reach, just in case!

2. Light the candle. Pick up your fabric swatch with the tweezers.

3. Bring the swatch over to the flame slowly. Once it starts to burn for a couple of seconds, continue to hold it over the tinfoil and slowly bring it away from the candle. Give the flames a chance to die down on their own.

4. Observe the way the fire behaves as it burns.

> *Does it ignite easily? Or does it curl up and shrink when it gets close to the flame?*
>
> *Does it melt or drip?*
>
> *Is there a flame or smoke? Is the smoke light or dark?*
>
> *Does the smell remind you of other burning materials such as hair or paper?*
>
> *Does the fire keep going when you remove it from the flame? Or does it extinguish by itself?*
>
> *What does the residue look like? When it's cool enough to touch, what does it feel like?*

Compare your findings to the chart of common fibres. If your fabric shares characteristics with more than one of these fibres, it may be a blend of two or more.

MIXED WOVEN FIBRES

If you suspect that a woven fabric is a blend, try separating the *warp* (vertical) and *weft* (horizontal) threads from each other with your fingers and testing them individually. Some mixed fibres have the warp and weft made from two different materials, and this may help you identify the individual fibres more accurately.

Fibre	Approaching flame	In flame	Removing from flame	Smell	Ashes or residue
Cotton (cellulose)	Ignites quickly	Burns rapidly with yellow flame	Continues to burn rapidly and smoke, glows	Burnt paper or leaves	Light, soft, grey*
Linen (cellulose)	Ignites quickly	Burns rapidly with yellow flame, slower than cotton	Continues to burn	Burnt paper	Light, soft, grey*
Rayon (cellulose)	Ignites quickly	Burns rapidly with yellow flame, faster than cotton	Continues to burn rapidly, does not glow	Burnt paper	Light, soft, grey
Silk (protein)	Shrinks away from flame	Burns slowly, sputters	Burns with difficulty, flame dies out	Burnt hair	Round black bead, brittle and crushable
Wool (protein)	Shrinks away from flame, slow to ignite	Burns slowly with small flame	Flame dies out	Strong burnt hair	Dark ash, irregular bead, brittle and crushable
Nylon (synthetic, also receptive to dyes for proteins)	Melts and shrinks away from flame	Melts, then slowly burns	Flame dies out	Celery	Round dark grey bead, hard and doesn't crush
Polyester (synthetic)	Melts and shrinks away from flame	Burns slowly with black smoke, melts	Burns with difficulty	Sweet, burnt plastic	Round black bead, hard and doesn't crush
Acetate (synthetic)	Melts, turns black	Burns rapidly with yellow flame, melts	Continues to burn and melt	Burnt paper, vinegar	Black ash, irregular bead, difficult to crush
Acrylic (synthetic)	Melts and shrinks away from flame	Burns rapidly, sputters	Continues to burn and melt	Fish, burnt plastic	Irregular black bead, hard and doesn't crush
Spandex (synthetic)	Melts and shrinks away from flame	Melts and burns	Continues to burn and melt	Bitter, sharp	Gummy and sticky

Ash from cotton or linen that has been mercerized (a chemical treatment that makes the fabric stronger, smoother, and more receptive to dye) may show up as black instead of grey.

The Right Dye for YOUR PROJECT

Just as there are different types of fibres, there are different types of dyes that work better on some fibres than others. These are a few of the most common types of dyes that cosplayers are likely to come across, from specially made chemicals to plants that have been used for centuries to drinks that you can find at a grocery store.

Even if they're meant to work on similar fibres, it's important to note that each brand of dye is different and you should always follow the manufacturer's instructions to get the best colour. For instance, some dye brands will require you to add table salt to your dye bath, while others may already have it mixed into the formula.

COSPLAYER: Marquise Cubey
COSTUME: Lup Taako Original Design inspired by *The Adventure Zone*
Photo by Lorna Phillips

Dye type	Best fibres	Okay fibres	Common brands
Union (a.k.a. multipurpose)	Cellulose blend Protein blend Nylon* Unknown fibre	Cellulose Protein Unknown fibre	Rit All-Purpose Dye Dylon Fabric Hand Dye Tintex Fabric Dye Jacquard iDye Tulip Fabric Dye
Disperse	Synthetic Unknown fibre	Synthetic blend Unknown fibre	Rit DyeMore Synthetic Dye Jacquard iDye Poly
Black tea	Cellulose Protein Nylon* Unknown fibre	Synthetic blend Cellulose blend Protein blend Unknown fibre	Different brands and blends can have slightly different results, so be sure to experiment!
Unsweetened drink mix	Protein Nylon*	Protein blend	Kool-Aid
Fibre reactive	Cellulose	Cellulose blend Protein Protein blend Nylon	Tulip One-Step Tie-Dye Tulip Two-Minute Tie-Dye Jacquard Procion MX Dharma Fiber Reactive Procion Dye
Direct	Cellulose	Cellulose blend	Dharma Hot Water Fiber Reactive Dye
Acid	Protein Nylon*	Protein blend	Jacquard Acid Dye Dharma Acid Dye Aljo Cotton and Rayon Dye

Nylon is a synthetic fibre, but it is unique in that it also takes dyes meant for protein fibres.

SAFETY FIRST!

Disperse dyes are the only option for synthetic fibres, and while the ones that come in liquid form are less tricky to work with safely than those in powder form, they can still be quite toxic and dangerous if not handled with care. Only use disperse dyes if you know from the very start that you cannot use anything else (such as when dyeing spandex or a synthetic wig), or if you have tried everything else. Just like any other chemical, make sure to look up the MSDS sheet for your dye. As a refresher on finding and using the MSDS, see Using Products and Materials Safely (page 16) before using it.

Beginner-Friendly Dyes

If you're a first-time dyer or you just have limited working space, you'll likely want to start your dyeing journey off with something that's easy and safer to use. Fortunately, there are plenty of great options that can be used in a wide variety of cosplay applications.

Liquid Dyes

Some union and disperse dyes are sold as bottled liquid solutions, such as Rit's line of liquid dyes, and these are some of the most popular and convenient dyes for cosplayers. Liquid dyes are generally easier to use than powdered dyes and can be safer than their powdered counterparts. When using disperse liquid dyes, be extra sure to have good ventilation. Liquid dyes can be a little bit more expensive than the same amount of pigment in powder form, but if you only need one or two bottles, the ease of use is absolutely worth the extra cost.

Black Tea

Many times, if you are looking to give something an aged look, you will often want to dye it slightly brown, and black tea is perfect for that. It's the safest to use, it can be used in your kitchen, it can be found at grocery stores, and to top it all off, it smells great too! The only downside is that it's not quite as predictable as traditional dyes, but it is absolutely the fastest.

Unsweetened Drink Mix

If you're looking to dye your fabric a bright colour and can only dye things in your kitchen, unsweetened drink mixes are an alternative to normal dyes. When drink mixes are used properly, they're just as colourfast and permanent as normal dyes. The colours can be limited, though, and drink mix dyes only work on protein fibres and nylon.

Kool-Aid is perhaps the most well-known brand of drink mix for dyeing, but other brands may be worth experimenting with as long as they have no added sugar and lots of food colouring.

Specialized Dyes

For the majority of cosplay dyeing, the beginner-friendly dyes outlined in the previous section are usually perfectly fine. However, they do have their limits, so sometimes you may want to turn to more specialized dyes for larger or more complex projects.

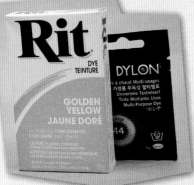

Powdered Dyes

The usual union and disperse dyes can sometimes be sold in a powdered form in addition to the liquid form, and specialized dyes almost always come in powders. This makes them easy to store and sometimes more economical than liquid dyes, which is awesome if you're dyeing yards and yards of fabric. They do require extra caution compared to liquid dyes, though, which makes them less ideal for casual dyers or those with limited workspaces.

Direct and Acid Dyes

These work pretty similarly to normal multipurpose union dyes (in fact, union dyes are made up of direct and acid dyes). However, direct dyes only work on cellulose fibres, and acid dyes only work on protein fibres and nylon.

In most cases, when you're dyeing just one garment or tweaking a colour, you'll generally be fine with regular all-purpose union dyes. However, if you're dyeing several yards of a known pure fibre a dark, saturated colour, direct and acid dyes can be a lifesaver because, on the right fibres, they can give much stronger colours in a smaller concentration for less money.

Fibre-Reactive Dyes

Unlike most of the dyes in this book, fibre-reactive dyes such as Jacquard's Procion MX and Tulip's line of tie-dye products do not require heat in order to work, making them perfect for multicolour dyeing, wax resists, and anything else that is difficult to do in a pot. Instead, a fixative chemical (usually soda ash dissolved in water) is applied to the fibre after dyeing and it is left to sit for several hours. Sometimes, you can even find convenient options that have soda ash already mixed in.

The main limitation of fibre-reactive dyes is that they only work on natural fibres and some only work on cellulose fibres. However, they are the brightest and longest-lasting dyes to use on cellulose fibres.

As of the time of writing, there are, sadly, no commercially available heat-free alternatives that bond to synthetic fibres (with the exception of nylon, of course), so if these dyes inspire you, make sure to choose the right fabrics.

Advanced Dyes and Colour Removers

While these aren't covered in detail in this book since they simply aren't practical for most cosplayers and projects, the more advanced side of textile arts is certainly worth at least an honourable mention. Some of these topics could fill an entire book of their own, so if they inspire you, they are absolutely worth researching.

FURTHER READING

One book in particular that I referred back to often during my research was *Fabric Painting and Dyeing for the Theatre* by Deborah M. Dryden, and I highly recommend it if you want to learn even more about how these more advanced dyes could be applied to costumes.

Natural Dyes

There are all kinds of natural dyes from indigo to cochineal, and many of them have been used around the world for centuries. Because they are natural, they usually have challenging quirks that aren't present in man-made dyes, including (but not limited to) giving you a completely different colour depending on the pH of your water. Despite this, or perhaps because of it, natural dyes are still beloved by the dedicated dyers who embrace these quirks, and as a result, they can be extremely satisfying to master.

Bleach and Discharge Agents

Discharge agents are a vast assortment of chemicals that remove (or, discharge) colour from fabric, including bleach. Unlike dyes, discharge chemicals can be highly unpredictable and hard to control with no two fabrics or dyes ever reacting in quite the same way, and they all have the potential to permanently damage your fibre. However, if you are using them in the context of weathering, this can actually be a feature, not a drawback, and can create really cool effects.

Unfortunately, discharge agents, including common household ones like bleach, are significantly less safe than you'd think, and even the most experienced career costume-breakdown artists I know would never use these chemicals in their houses or without the most intense PPE money can buy. Not only are discharge chemicals themselves harmful, but when colour is removed from fabric, the pigment doesn't disappear. Instead, it gets broken down into other chemical compounds, which are often airborne and almost always far more dangerous than the pigment was before, and many of them are known carcinogens.

With all of that being said, if you happen to be lucky enough to have access to the proper equipment and space to work in, I actually highly encourage you to keep learning about discharge agents because they are absolutely fascinating. Experts have written books and dissertations about how to use these chemicals and how to use them safely, and they can be an invaluable resource.

Materials and Tools
FOR DYEING

Now that you have chosen your fabric and your dye, you're going to have to get some tools in order. Fortunately, for most of your dyeing needs, the vast majority of the materials you'll need are normal, inexpensive kitchen items that can be easily found at grocery, dollar, or thrift stores.

COSPLAYER: Marquise Cubey
COSTUME: Little Sister from *Bioshock 2*
Photo by John Rotor–Murphy

Consumable Products

Dye can't stick to fibre all on its own, so these products are must-haves in every dyer's toolkit.

Table salt is added to pretty much every dye bath in order to help the dye stick better to the fibre. You will often need to add an entire cup of it at a time to a bath, so it may be wise to buy extra.

Synthrapol is a special detergent by Jacquard that is really, really good at both washing excess dye out of hand-dyed fabrics and at locking in the colour that you actually want to stay in. Seriously, this stuff is basically magic and I never dye anything without it.

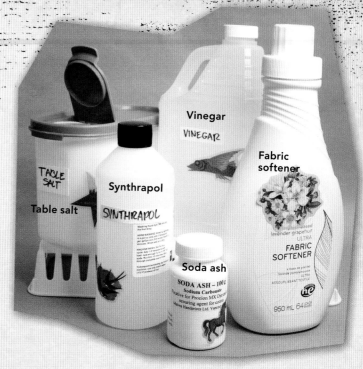

Household vinegar is added to dye baths when dyeing protein fibres and nylon.

Soda ash (optional) is a white chemical powder with a variety of uses in both dyeing and weathering, most notably as the fixative chemical for fibre-reactive dyes. If dye isn't sticking evenly to a cellulose fibre, you can also scour it beforehand by boiling it in a pot of water with soda ash. Soda ash is toxic stuff, though, so make sure to read the safety information thoroughly before deciding whether to use it.

Fabric softener (optional) is handy if you're dyeing a long wig. Wigs can tangle a fair amount during the dyeing process, and spraying fabric softener on a wig after you're done will make it easier to detangle.

Measuring Tools

These tools are handy for measuring weights, liquids, and time.

Keep a variety of measuring cups and spoons on hand. Different amounts of fabric require different amounts of dye, so you're going to need some of these.

SAFETY FIRST!

Unless it is otherwise specified, you must have separate kitchen utensils and containers specifically for dyeing. As soon as you use a kitchen item for chemicals, it is considered contaminated and you can't use it for food any longer. Don't use your grandma's favourite soup pot!

GO METRIC

If you are able to find them, use measuring tools that include metric measurements, showing weight in grams and liquid volume in millilitres.

Non-sterile *syringes* (without needles) are perfect for measuring small, precise quantities of dye. These can usually be bought over the counter at the pharmacy for small change. Having several on hand in different sizes such as 5ml and 10ml is quite handy, especially for when you're mixing dye colours.

Digital kitchen scales with metric values are perfect for measuring fibre and dye weights when doing precise colour matching and testing. This is one of the very few tools where you don't need to buy a new one just to use it with dye, simply cover it with plastic wrap to protect it, and clean it off with a damp, soapy cloth when you are finished.

A *calculator* is useful when figuring out how much dye to use, as there is some math involved in the process.

A *kitchen timer* is an important tool to have on hand so that you can keep track of how long your fibre has been in your dye bath. Personally, I like using a voice-activated assistant such as Siri to set and check timers so that I don't have to keep removing my gloves.

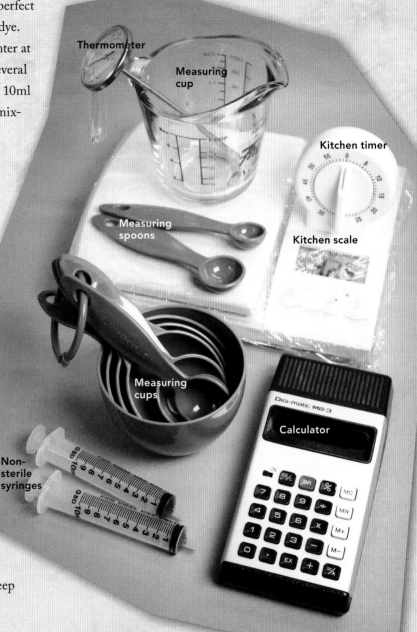

Thermometer

Measuring cup

Kitchen timer

Measuring spoons

Kitchen scale

Measuring cups

Non-sterile syringes

Calculator

Plastic tub

Stirring utensils

Electric kettle

Dye pot

Electric hot plate

Immersion Dyeing Tools

These are all the larger tools that you will need when dyeing. It may seem like a lot to buy at first, especially considering you can't reuse them for food. Fortunately, though, most of these can be found easily and cheaply at thrift stores, especially the cooking pots.

A metal *dye pot* is great for when you need to heat up your dye bath for darker and more saturated colours. Make sure to get a big one so it can hold all of your fabric with plenty of room to swish around.

A *plastic bucket or tub* can be an alternative to a metal dye pot for when you are dyeing lighter or more subtle colours that don't need a heat source. Large plastic storage containers are also amazing for when you are dyeing large quantities of fabric or if you are gradient dyeing.

A *portable electric hot plate* or *camp stove* is great for dyeing dark colours outdoors or in the garage. Dyeing is a messy endeavour, and you may not always want to use dye (a.k.a. a chemical whose sole purpose is to

permanently stain things weird colours) inside your nice kitchen.

SAFETY FIRST!
Only operate propane camp stoves outdoors! Propane gives off carbon monoxide gas when it burns, which can become deadly if it fills up a room.

Stirring utensils such as wooden takeout chopsticks are perfect for mixing and dissolving dyes, and larger wooden cooking spoons are great for stirring a larger dye bath.

An *electric kettle (optional)* is useful to quickly boil water for mixing and diluting dye, though if you don't have one, boiling water in a pot on the stove also works just fine. This is another kitchen item that you do not have to purchase specifically for dye since only water ever goes in or out.

Dyeing Based on *FIBRE WEIGHT*

When using any sort of dye, it's very tempting to just dump the entire contents of the bottle or packet into your dye bath, throw your garment or wig in, and pray to Zeus that you get a colour that looks good, taking it out when it gets dark enough for your liking. And sometimes, if you're not picky and are just eyeballing the colour until it looks good, this is a perfectly fine way to get results.

However, for projects that require more accuracy, it can make testing on swatches difficult, and that can lead to unexpected colour results that are difficult to reverse. Additionally, it can be wasteful if you aren't yet sure how much dye to use, and if you take the fibre out too early, the dye may not have had a chance to bond completely, which can lead to colours bleeding.

Fortunately, by learning to dye your fibre based on weight, you will be able to test for precise colours with ease and even predict more accurately how they will turn out, opening yourself up to so many more colour possibilities!

METRIC MALARKEY

Something that you will notice very quickly is that many of the numbers in the remaining dyeing chapters are written using the metric system. This is for the same reason you use the metric system in chemistry class: It just makes the math a whole lot simpler.

I want this book to be as inclusive as possible, so even though the metric system is how I and the majority of industry dyers work, I still tried to see if there was any way to create a U.S. equivalent. However, in practice, I very quickly discovered that the traditional U.S. measurement system works best when measuring things that relate to humans, such as food portions, but is more difficult to work with when you are dealing with percentages as you generally do when dyeing.

The good news is, even if you are used to working in U.S. measurement units, tools used to measure precise amounts such as syringes already display metric units no matter what, even in the United States. Additionally, if you are used to the U.S. system and need a quick review on what metric units look like, there is a super handy Metric Conversion Chart (page 125) that you can use as a refresher.

Depth of Shade

When figuring out how much dye to use for a project, you need to know two important factors going in: how much fibre you are dyeing and how deep you want your colour to be.

The amount of dye you need to colour any fibre is based on how much your dry fibre weighs in grams. As you would expect, this can be measured simply by weighing it on a standard scale. To make things easier to write, we can call this the *weight of fibre*, or WOF for short.

The second factor is called the *depth of shade*, or DOS for short. Since you are trying to take the abstract concept of how deep you want a colour to be and translate it into a practical amount of dye to use, it makes sense to think of depth of shade as the amount of dye you're using (in millilitres) per gram of fibre. So, a DOS of 1% means that for every 1g of material, you are adding 1mL of liquid dye to your dye bath.

A 2% DOS means there is 2mL of dye for every 1g of material, 0.5% DOS means there is 0.5mL for every 1g, and so on. More dye means a darker colour, so if you want your colour to be twice as dark, you simply add twice as much.

The best thing about measuring your dye this way is that it doesn't matter whether you're dyeing a tiny swatch or 3 whole yards of fabric, the same DOS on the same fibre will give you pretty much the same colour every time, making test swatches super easy to replicate, even days later.

What Do Different Depths of Shade Look Like?

Generally, anything under 1% DOS will result in a light colour, with 0.5% being a good starting point. A DOS of 0.25% is even more subtle and is useful when tweaking a colour rather than changing it altogether. Colours under a 1% concentration also don't need as much heat to bond properly since there is less dye, so you can dye them in a regular plastic bucket with warm tap water.

Colours over 1% DOS, on the other hand, can range from medium to dark. With the exception of fibre-reactive dyes, the dyes have to be encouraged with heat since there's more pigment. Medium to dark colours are almost always done in a pot on a stove or hot plate, and they can be so satisfying to get just right.

Depth of shade is also based on the total amount of all the dyes you are using in that particular dye bath. So, if you wanted to dye something with a DOS of 3% and mix two colours in a 1:2 ratio, you would mix together the dye needed for a 1% DOS of colour A with the dye needed for a 2% DOS of colour B before adding it to the water.

DYEING STRONG COLOURS

Generally, you won't find yourself going anywhere near or above a 10% DOS very often. If you are doing tests with union dyes and you find that you are approaching a high DOS in order to get the colour you need, consider using a more specialised dye such as acid or fibre reactive to get more bang for your buck, as they are much stronger on pure natural fibres.

Testing and Experimenting

Dye tests are done with small swatches of the fabric you plan to dye before you dye a larger amount of the fabric. It can sometimes take a few tests to find just the right colour, but it can be immensely rewarding to get it perfect, especially if you are dyeing to match another fabric or your skin tone.

Just like a science experiment, you'll want to record every possible factor that might affect your end product so that you're ready to replicate it flawlessly when the time comes to dye the real thing. Here is an example of a table you can use while doing dye tests. A blank Dye Test Results Template can be found at the end of the book (page 124).

Weight of fibre (WOF)	Dye concentration (%)	Colour ratio	Salt added(mL)	Other added (mL)	Time	Water temp.	Finished sample

Generally, you want test swatches small enough that you don't waste fabric, but large enough that you can weigh and measure dye for them easily. For a medium-weight fabric, I like to cut my test swatches as 2″ × 12″ (5cm × 30cm) strips. If you are dyeing a very lightweight fabric such as chiffon or tulle, cut your swatches twice as wide so they are easier to weigh.

BLACK

While on the topic of dark colours, it should be noted that it is, unfortunately, very, very difficult to dye any fibres perfectly black in a nonindustrial setting. While black dyes for home use exist, they are often more practical for dyeing dark, cool greys or for mixing with other colours. You can, in theory, dye something black multiple times to get a darker colour, but this can get expensive and there may be so much dye in your fibre that it will begin to rub off on things.

If you are making a wig with a black gradient or ombre, you may be better off buying black wefts and sewing them in strategically rather than attempting to dye the wig. That being said, if your cosplay's fabric needs a black ombre and you can't avoid dip-dyeing it, you could dye it at the dark end of the gradient and then manually paint in a darker hue using a large brush and black fabric ink or watered-down paint on wet fabric.

DYEING WITH BLACK TEA

hile not quite as colourfast as proper dyes, black tea is a great quick-and-dirty way to subtly dye many fibres, either for weathering purposes or to tone down the colour. Since tea dyeing is just meant to be a way to weather something, your DOS isn't as important as it is for more precise chemical dyeing. Instead, the amount of time you leave something in a tea dye bath is the more important factor.

That being said, in order to keep things consistent between swatches and the real fabric, it's good to use a consistent amount of tea in relation to the weight of fibre. In the example below, I dyed my fibre with an amount of tea equal to 5% WOF just because it was easy to measure, but you can use any amount as long as everything stays proportional.

MATERIALS

Fibre for dyeing

Boiling water

Black tea bags, roughly equal to 5% WOF

TOOLS AND EQUIPMENT

Apron

Rubber gloves

Kitchen scale

Calculator

Notepad and pen

Glass pitcher or large bowl

Cotton dyed in orange pekoe tea for 10 minutes

Process

To give tea dyeing a try, follow these steps.

1. Weigh the fibre that you plan to dye and record the WOF in grams.

2. Divide your WOF by 20 to get your 5%. Place teabags on the scale until the weight of the teabags is equal to this number in grams.

Example: If you are dyeing 500g of fabric with black tea, your math should look like this: 500g ÷ 20 = 25g of tea.

3. In the glass pitcher or bowl, pour boiling water over your teabags. Let them steep for 10 minutes.

4. Remove the teabags with a spoon. Use your tea solution to dye your fabric à la Dyeing Solid Colours (page 62) on the same day that you made it.

MAKING A LIQUID SOLUTION FROM A POWDERED DYE

Powdered dyes are toxic and require caution when dissolving into a solution, but the advantages of being able to access the diverse world of dyes that only come in powder form can be worth it. You can use this exact same process (with slightly less intense safety measures) to dissolve unsweetened drink mixes for dyeing, which can be stored in the fridge for up to five days.

MATERIALS

Package or container of powdered dye

500mL (16 fl. oz.) jar (holds a 1% solution for a package of dye weighing 5g or less)

Hot water

Paper towels

TOOLS AND EQUIPMENT

Apron or old clothes

Chemical-resistant rubber gloves

Safety goggles

Cartridge respirator (with *particulate* filters installed) or a properly fitted N95 dust mask

Spoon

Measuring cup

Stirring utensils

Kitchen scale covered in plastic wrap

Calculator

Notepad and pen

SAFETY FIRST!

Fabric dye is toxic, so you will need to take extra safety measures to make sure you don't accidentally breathe in stray powder and to clean it up extremely well with a wet paper towel afterward so that there are no traces of dry dye left. If you don't have access to a properly ventilated workspace and the required PPE, it is best to reconsider using powdered dye and look into safer (and more convenient) liquid options instead.

DYE BOX

If you own the appropriate tools, you can make a see-through box, with holes cut out for your hands, to keep dye powder contained. Working underneath a box like this means that you can mix dye in a regular ventilated space indoors, and it eliminates the need for a dust mask and goggles (though you will still have to wear gloves and clean up very well afterward).

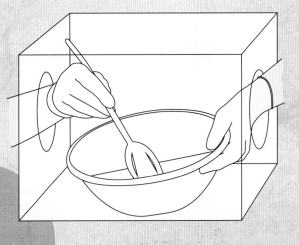

Process

Some powdered dyes are sold in small packets, while others are sold in larger tins or jars. For each type of packaging, there are different tricks you can use to safely dissolve the dye.

Using Small Dye Packets

If your dye comes in small dye packets, follow these steps.

1. Check the weight of the packet and use a calculator to convert it to grams if needed. Multiply the weight of the powder by 100. Measure out this amount of hot water in millilitres and pour it into the jar (for example, for a 4.3g package, you need 430mL of hot water).

2. Pour some of the water from your jar into the measuring cup. Add the powder to the water in the cup and stir until dissolved. Do not throw out the package just yet.

3. Dip the empty package into the measuring cup and swirl it around with gloved hands, making sure all of the dye gets out of the package and into the water so that there is no dry powder left inside.

Using Dye from a Larger Container

When your dye comes in a larger container, follow these steps to create a solution.

1. Measure out 500mL of hot water and pour it into the jar.

2. Place your measuring cup onto the kitchen scale and calibrate it to the weight of the cup. (This function may work differently on different scales, so familiarize yourself with this feature on your scale.) While wearing all of the appropriate PPE, use a small spoon to scoop very small amounts of dye into the measuring cup until the scale reads 5g in total.

3. Pour some of the water from your jar into the measuring cup. Stir until dissolved.

Finishing

1. Pour the solution back into the jar and mix it all together with a spoon.

2. Clean up your workstation using a wet paper towel and rinse out your measuring cup very well. Once all of the dye has been cleaned up, you may finally remove your mask and eye protection.

3. Label your container with the colour name, the brand, the concentration (in our case, 1%), and today's date.

Your chemical dye solution can be kept in the container for up to one year before it expires, and drink-mix solutions can be kept in the fridge for up to five days. If you don't end up using it all on your project, you may be able to use it again on a different one.

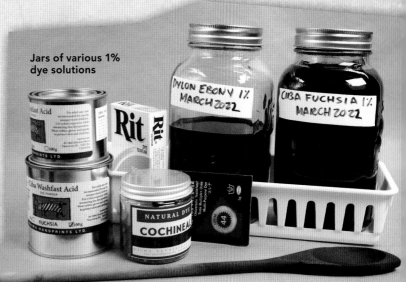

Jars of various 1% dye solutions

Dyeing Solid
COLOURS

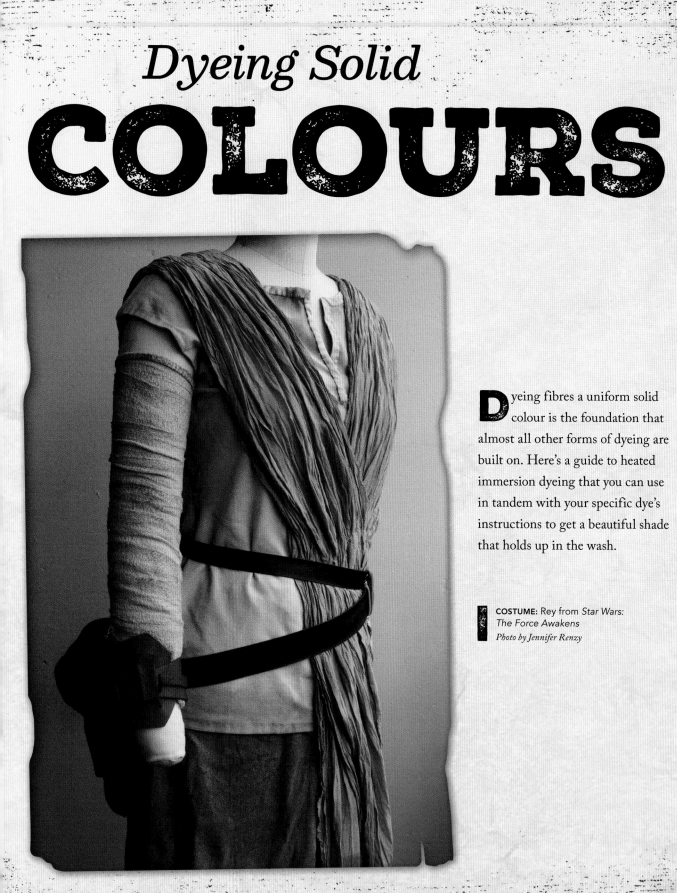

Dyeing fibres a uniform solid colour is the foundation that almost all other forms of dyeing are built on. Here's a guide to heated immersion dyeing that you can use in tandem with your specific dye's instructions to get a beautiful shade that holds up in the wash.

COSTUME: Rey from *Star Wars: The Force Awakens*
Photo by Jennifer Renzy

DYEING FIBRE A SOLID COLOR

Process

To dye your fibre in an immersion dye bath, follow these steps.

1. Weigh your *dry* fibre on the scale and record the fibre weight (WOF) in grams.

2. Prep your fibre. Dye can only work on fibre if it can actually reach it, and any factory treatments, oils, dust, or surface finishes could get in the way. For most fibres, simply prewash in warm water with Synthrapol or laundry soap to prep them. For protein fibres, use a neutral or gentle soap meant for wool.

MATERIALS

Fibre for dyeing

Dye in a liquid solution (Note: This specific process is not meant for fibre-reactive dyes; for those, I recommend sticking with the dye's recommended instructions.)

Table salt

Household vinegar (if dyeing a protein fibre)

Synthrapol or laundry soap

Fabric softener (if dyeing a long wig)

TOOLS AND EQUIPMENT

Apron

Chemical-resistant rubber gloves

Bucket, bowl, or pot (large enough to hold all of your fibre)

Kitchen scale

Syringes

Measuring cup

Stirring utensils

Calculator

Notepad and a pen

Hair dryer (if dyeing test swatches or dyeing something for the first time)

Kitchen timer

SCOURING: WHEN WASHING ISN'T ENOUGH

If you've done dye tests after washing your fibre and the dye is still not sticking in the way you hoped it would, try scouring. Some cellulose fibres can seriously benefit from a scour in addition to a regular wash before dyeing. *Scouring* is the textile term for boiling a fibre in a pot of water with laundry soap, and it can be really effective for removing stubborn factory grunge.

If you need to scour your fabric, you can search online for "how to scour (fibre name)" and find tutorials on exactly how to do it so that the fibre doesn't get damaged by the heat. Every fibre is different and some may even require you to mix in other substances such as soda ash or Synthrapol.

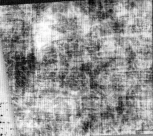

An example of some cotton dyed with natural indigo without scouring (left) and after scouring (right).

3. Fill a pot with enough water to cover the fibre. Turn on the heat, and monitor the temperature. Every dye has a recommended dye bath temperature, so be sure to consult the instructions that came with the one you're using. If you can't find this info, 150°F–170°F (65°C–75°C) is usually a safe place to be.

As a general rule, try to keep your dye bath as close to the minimum required temperature as you can. This is especially important for fibres that are sensitive to excessive heat such as silk, wool, or plastic so they don't get scorched, felted, or warped.

DYEING WITHOUT A STOVE

If you are dyeing a natural fibre a light colour with a 1% DOS or less, use an unheated dye bath. Simply replace the pot on the stove with a large dye-only bowl or bucket filled with enough warm water to cover the fibre.

4. Use a calculator to multiply the weight of your dry fibre by your desired DOS. This is the amount of dye in millilitres that you will need. For example, if you are dyeing 352g of fibre at a 0.5% DOS (352 × 0.5 = 176), you will need to measure out 176mL of liquid dye.

5. Wearing rubber gloves and an apron, use a syringe to measure the amount of dye that you need, and keep it in the measuring cup.

6. Add boiling water to the measuring cup containing your dye, and stir. There doesn't need to be an exact amount of boiling water, but it should be enough to heat up the dye and help it fully dissolve.

7. Add the dye to the larger pot or bowl of water, along with the required amounts of salt and vinegar recommended by the dye manufacturer in the dye instructions. The salt and vinegar adjust the pH of the water, so you don't need to calculate them based on the weight of the fibre.

If you're using tea or drink mix and don't have this information, you can use 250g (1 cup) of salt and 150mL (⅔ cup) of vinegar when dyeing proteins and nylon.

SALT AND VINEGAR

If dye instructions do not specify adding salt, this is often because the salt is already in the dye formula itself. However, adding some vinegar when dyeing protein fibres never hurts (even if the instructions don't say specifically to do so), especially if you have hard tap water.

8. Wet your fibre with warm water if it isn't already wet from washing. If you are dyeing wool, which is very sensitive to sudden shifts in temperature, to avoid damage, wet it first with lukewarm water and then with hot water so the temperature shift is more gradual.

9. Add the fibre to the dye bath and set a timer for 10–15 minutes. If you are dyeing test swatches, start running the kitchen timer or take note of the current time so you'll know how long to leave it in for the real thing.

Stir the fibre around consistently with a large utensil, opening it up so that the dye can get into every crevice and fold.

10. Once the timer goes off, check your fibre's colour. To more accurately check the colour, use a hair dryer to dry a small section of your fibre to see what it looks like.

11. If you are satisfied with the colour, remove it from the dye bath. If you think your colour should be darker, leave it in the pot for up to 45 additional minutes until you reach the desired shade, stirring occasionally.

12. Turn off the heat and use a spoon or heat-resistant rubber gloves to remove the fibre from the dye bath. Rinse the fibre in cool water. If you are dyeing wool, make sure to start with warm water and gradually lower the temperature to avoid shocking it.

13. Wash the fibre with Syn-thrapol or laundry detergent until the water runs clear.

14. If you are dyeing a long wig, wet it with fabric softener and gently begin combing it out, starting from the bottom and working your way up.

15. Hang your fibre up to dry and clean up your workspace, utensils, and sink.

Creating Patterns and Texture

WITH DYE

As you may be aware, dye doesn't just have to be used to change a fibre's colour in a uniform way. This chapter expands on basic dyeing methods, showing how to get unique patterns in your fabric that are only possible with dye. The best part is that all of the techniques touched on in this chapter can be combined with each other, and the possibilities are endless!

Resist Dyeing

We know already that in order to get a solid colour, we need to open up a fibre so that the dye can reach it all, but what if we decided to do the opposite on purpose? Dye can't get onto a fibre if something is in its way, and that's where the concept of resist dyeing comes in.

A *resist* is essentially any kind of dye blocker. To use any one of these resist-dyeing methods, you would start by applying a resist to your fabric and then dye it normally as though it were a solid colour.

COSPLAYER: CocoaSugarCosplay
COSTUME: Anthy from original fan art by Dessi_Desu, inspired by *Revolutionary Girl Utena*
Photo by Felix Dandy

Tied Resist

Commonly called *tie-dyeing*, this is likely the form of resist dyeing you're most familiar with. The method is in the name. After prewashing your fibre and before putting it in your dye bath, tightly bind sections of the fibre or garment you are dyeing with string, rope, or rubber bands.

Any portion of the fibre or garment that is bound will show as a stripe in the original colour, and the tighter you bind, the bolder the stripes!

Stitched Resist

Commonly known as *shibori dyeing*, this is a variation on tie-dyeing that involves using a thick needle and thread to gather fabric into more intricate shapes, and it shows up in traditional dress all across Asia and Africa. There are entire books on shibori dyeing, but to give it a try, select a needle size that is slightly larger than you'd normally use on your intended fabric and a thick, sturdy thread. Stitch patterns across the surface of your fabric, pulling the threads to tightly bunch up the fabric under your stitches. Dye as normal and see what happens! To get a specific pattern, search online and you'll find tons of shibori tutorials. While it can be time consuming, if you want to really go in depth with something like kimono fabric, it could be really cool to learn.

Clamped Resist

This involves sandwiching fabric between two shaped plates and clamping them together. Because the dye does not reach that area of the fabric, it remains the colour of the original material. These plates are often made from wood, but they can be made out of anything as long as they won't warp at your dye bath's temperature. To give this a try, select two plates of the same shape, then fold your fabric up so that it is slightly larger than your selected plates. Place the folded fabric between the two plates and clamp them together using any clamp that will not melt or warp in your dye bath. Dye as normal and check out the results.

3D-PRINTED PLATES

If you have a 3D printer, you can use it to make clamp resist plates in any shape you need. Just be sure to use a filament that can stand higher temperatures, such as ABS.

Organic Resist

To get an organic resist, all you need to do is crumple your fibre into a ball and leave it in your dye bath without stirring. This can create some really cool natural textures, and it's great for all kinds of characters from woodsy fairies to spooky monsters.

Wax Resist

Also known as *batik dyeing*, this involves heating up wax and drawing patterns onto fabric with it, dyeing, then cleaning it off afterward. You can use special batik wax or wax resist sticks if you're a purist; however, if you're on a budget, you can actually use washable gel craft glue instead of wax, and it works just as well. Just leave it to dry overnight before dunking it in dye.

It's important to note that not all wax resists can survive a hot dye bath, so they may be best suited for light colours or fibre-reactive dyes. Make sure the resist covers both sides of the fibre. When you're finished dyeing, all you need to do after rinsing out your excess dye is to remove the wax by ironing it out or by heating the fabric in a pot of hot water until the wax dissolves.

Painted Dyeing

It is possible to apply fibre-reactive dyes (page 46) to natural fibres with brushes as though they were ink or paint. Use either a squeeze bottle or a paintbrush with natural bristles to apply the dye to fabric that's either sitting flat on a large drop cloth or bound with resists. Follow the instructions for your dye so it can bond properly. This technique is great for achieving everything from watercolour-like patterns to discoloured weathered-fabric effects.

Dip-Dyeing

Dip-dyeing, also known as *ombre* or *gradient dyeing*, is perhaps the most popular thing that attracts cosplayers to dyeing, whether it's for wigs or fabric. A dip-dyed fabric or item gradually fades from one colour into the dyed colour, which can be handy when weathering something, whether for adding a definitive stain or just some visual interest.

Dip-dyeing is not only awesome for weathering, but it's popular in a ton of fantastical designs. It's a versatile effect and, for extra visual interest and drama, can be added to all kinds of things like skirts, capes, gloves, wigs, and linings, just to name a few!

MATERIALS

Fibre for dyeing

Dye (in a liquid solution)

Table salt

Household vinegar (if dyeing a protein fibre)

Synthrapol or laundry soap

Rubber bands and/or some string (if dyeing a wig or an assembled garment)

Chalk and/or safety pins (if dyeing an assembled garment)

TOOLS AND EQUIPMENT

Apron

Chemical-resistant rubber gloves

Bucket, bowl, or pot (large enough to hold fibre)

Kitchen scale

Syringes

Measuring cup

Stirring utensils

Calculator

Notepad and pen

Hair dryer (optional)

Kitchen timer

Process

How you plan out your dip-dyeing depends on whether you are dyeing raw materials or finished garments and wigs.

For Yardage, Rectangular Pieces of Fabric, and Wig Wefts

When dyeing materials with little variation in cut, density, and weight distribution, follow these steps.

1. Weigh your dry fibre on the scale and record the total WOF in grams.

2. In order to know how much dye you need, you must decide how much of your fibre you want your colour to cover and mark approximately where you want the colour to stop with a pin. Estimate how that will affect your WOF.

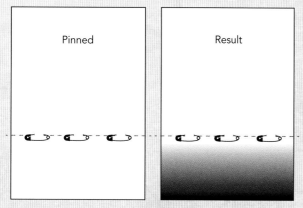

For instance, if you only wish to dye about one-third of a 600g piece of fabric, you can estimate that the WOF to be dyed is approximately 200g.

For Fully Assembled Garments and Wigs

If you are dying something already made, these are the steps to follow.

1. On your dry garment or wig, mark approximately where you want your colour to stop using a safety pin, tailors' chalk, or by tying it with string.

If the section you have marked to be dyed is larger than your scale's weighing surface, fold it into a ball or braid it and secure it loosely with string so that it doesn't fall apart.

2. Place the fibre partially on the scale so that only the part that you want to dye is on the weighing surface. Record this approximate weight of WOF in grams.

For All Fibres

Now that you've marked the area to be dyed, follow these steps regardless of whether you are dyeing raw materials or finished pieces.

3. Follow steps 2 through 7 of Dyeing Solid Colours (page 62) to prepare your fibre and dye bath.

4. For 15–20 minutes, dip the fibre in and out of the bath up to where you have marked, being sure to open the fabric up in the water as you would when dyeing a solid colour. The part of the garment that will be darkest should spend the most time in the dye bath, while the lighter transition parts should spend less time in. Keep moving the fibre up and down so that the colour can fade smoothly.

SMOOTHER TRANSITIONS

If you find that your colour isn't fading as smoothly as you'd like it to, spray the top of your gradient with water to help the colour bleed downwards.

For dip-dyeing, you will often be eyeballing the colour until it looks good since your WOF is only approximate. The colour can be quickly checked by drying it with a hair dryer as you go.

5. When the time is up, turn off the heat if you are using a heated dye bath. For a brighter and more colourfast dye job, keep dipping the fibre in the bath for an additional 10 minutes.

6. When you are happy with your shade, remove your fibre and wash it out with Synthrapol or laundry soap until the water runs clear.

7. Optional: To add additional colours, simply rinse the previously dyed area out as you normally would, make a new dye bath, and repeat, again moving the fibre up and down so that the colours bleed together.

COSPLAYER: Lutavia Cosplay
COSTUME: San from *Princess Mononoke*
Photo by Jonathan Vilches

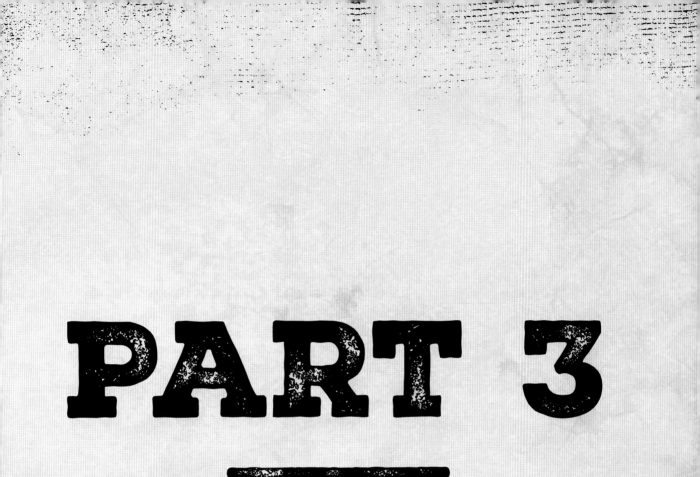

PART 3

THE BEAUTY OF DESTRUCTION

Building Costumes to Be
DESTROYED

T he fun secret about building costumes that you are going to weather heavily is that you don't need to worry about everything looking beautiful and straight, even if it's a contest piece that you're putting a ton of time into. However, there are some things that you may want to approach differently than normal when putting together a costume that's going to be physically distressed.

COSPLAYER: Vic Treviño
COSTUME: Vicar Amelia from *Bloodborne*
Photo by David Ngo

Hems

If you're planning on ripping a hem to shreds, you can often get away with leaving it unhemmed until it's time to tear it up.

A Vicar Amelia's dress before weathering. Notice how the overskirt has been finished with lace, but the underskirt's hem is left raw.

B The underskirt for Vicar Amelia's dress after weathering. This layer drags on the ground, so it makes sense for it to be the most shredded part of the dress.

Photos by Vic Treviño

It can also look interesting if you finish the hem normally and leave some parts intact, especially if your hem is on a structured garment such as a coat.

C The Little Sister's dress before physical weathering with a finished hem at the bottom. The skirt was also made two inches longer than I would normally make a knee-length skirt, since the process of shredding it would make it appear shorter.

D The Little Sister's dress after physical weathering. The bits of the hem that were left intact help to ground the raggedy dress in reality and give it a history, as well as some visual interest.

Seam Finishes

If you plan to add holes or rips near seams or hems, you will be able to see your seam finishes, or lack of seam finishes. This doesn't necessarily mean that the seams need to look beautiful—in fact, they'll be getting messed up later anyway—but it does mean that they should look in character, or at least not stand out too much. For instance, if you normally overlock or zigzag all of your raw edges, consider whether a modern, machine-sewn finish would look out of place when exposed. If so, you may not want to finish your raw edge at all.

KEEPING IT TOGETHER

To make up for the lost structural integrity from physical weathering, be sure to finish the seams on the parts of your garment that won't have holes torn into them.

Interfacing and Internal Structure

If you've ever used a large piece of iron-on cotton interfacing on fabric and forgotten to preshrink your materials, you may be familiar with the unfortunate rippled texture that can result from washing your finished fused piece in hot water. In the context of weathering, however, this can actually create a really cool textured effect. To achieve this effect on purpose, be sure not to prewash your selected fabric before applying the iron-on cotton interfacing. When your piece is complete, wash in hot water.

This dress was washed in hot water and the cotton interfacing on the white section shrank as a result.

As with seam finishes, you might want to think more about the type of interfacing you use since it may actually be seen if you plan on putting in holes. I like using woven interfacings because they behave more like fabric and have a nice, organic-looking texture, but something else may work better for your character. If you really want to go off the rails and look otherworldly or futuristic, you could even try using an unusually coloured fabric as sewn-in interfacing.

This sleeve's cuff was torn open, revealing the woven interfacing on the inside.

Texture and FADING

This level of weathering is subtle, but it shouldn't be underestimated. Even if it's not as flashy as big rips or zombie blood-stains, adding physical texture and fading to a weathered costume before adding the less subtle effects adds that je ne sais quoi. Even if you don't notice it at first, your brain does, and it helps to tell a story by building the effects one atop the other. It's great for making a weathered costume look lived in and naturally worn, and on heavily weathered cosplays, it creates a unified texture that can sometimes make extreme elements look even better.

COSPLAYER: Lutavia Cosplay
COSTUME: Bela Dimitrescu from *Resident Evil Village*
Photo by Yinyue Photography

Overall Wear

A great way to get an overall weathered foundation and mitigate some fabric waste is by using recycled fabric for your initial materials. An even simpler method is to create your cosplay from modified secondhand clothing since the wear is already present.

However, if you're making your garment completely from scratch, you might be able to substitute old bedsheets from the thrift store for new fabric. The colour of used fabric may not be uniform due to real breakdown, so you may have to go in afterward and manually touch things up if the colour difference is too stark for your liking.

WHAT CAN I MAKE WITH A BEDSHEET?

A standard queen-sized single-layer sheet is roughly equivalent to 4 yards (3.6m) of 60˝ (150cm)-wide fabric, approximately enough for an entire long-sleeved floor-length robe!

If you're weathering something that you've made from scratch or bought new, simply washing your garment in hot water and throwing in a couple of dishwashing scouring pads, available at most dollar stores, is a good way to speed up wear and tear that might normally take months of washing. If you have a machine dryer, you can also throw the garment in there with the scouring pads and some dryer balls to further enhance the effect. We've all heard of stonewashed jeans, one of the most common examples of intentionally weathered clothing. This does work, but it is better to do this by hand in a tub and not with your good washer, as true stonewashing can damage your washing machine.

Adding Wear in Specific Areas

Plain fabric

Fabric sanded with coarse-grit sandpaper

Sandpaper is one of the most common physical weathering tools used in film and theatre costumes, and it's an easy, quick way to rough up anything you can think of.

Coarse-grit sandpaper will generally tear up your fabric more and pull at threads, while fine-grit sandpaper will soften it up and fade the colour. Since every fabric is different, having a variety of sandpaper grits on hand is awesome so that you can experiment.

Fabric sanded with fine-grit sandpaper

A sanded texture works great on high-traffic areas. For an overview of which areas are most natural-looking with wear jump back to Fading and Physical Wear (page 30).

Sanding is also very effective at accentuating design elements such as seams and gathers. To make wrinkles and gathers stand out more, scrunch your fabric together in the same way that it would naturally bunch up while being worn. Sand across the top of the gathered fabric with finer grit sandpaper.

FADED, NOT FALLING APART
Make sure not to sand so much that it compromises the structure of the garment. If your texture from sanding is more noticeable with your eyes than with a camera, keep in mind that you can always make it pop more by dry brushing over it with paint. To learn how, check out Dry Brushing and Shading (page 32).

Sanding on top of gathered fabric

Finished result

LEATHER VS. SYNTHETICS

Genuine leather softens up and fades really nicely when sanded, and it generally looks the way you'd expect beat-up, older leather to look. While plant-based alternatives like vegetable-tanned leather or pineapple leather will generally break down nicely, most of the less expensive leather alternatives are actually a plastic lamination adhered to a fabric backing. Because the leather effect is only a surface layer, any sanding and weathering is more likely to appear chipped and scratched, which may not be the look you want.

While this does mean that you are sometimes limited in terms of physical weathering when using pleather and vinyl, the good thing is that much of the fading that is actually noticeable can be replicated with light and dark paints, as long as you have a reference to check your colours against. See Painting Pleather and Leather (page 97) for tips on how to make synthetics look a little more like aged leather.

COSPLAYER: Alexandra Hudson
COSTUME: Original Character inspired by *Star Wars*
Photography by David Ngo

Visible
REPAIRS

Decorative patches and cosmetic darning are one of the few truly reversible ways to add textured weathering to a cosplay costume, and they are also some of my personal favourites in general. This chapter includes a few ideas for visually interesting repairs that you can use as a jumping-off point for your character.

COSPLAYER: Marquise Cubey
COSTUME: Gina Lestrade from *The Great Ace Attorney*
Photography by John Rotor-Murphy

The use of mismatched darning threads and patterned scraps on the elbow and knee patches help bring a whole new layer of depth and whimsy to Gina's otherwise simple character design.

Hand-Sewing Tips for Weathering

To add any of these fake repairs, you will need some hand-sewing tools, including needles, scissors, and a thimble if your fabric is thick. To help your work stand out, use embroidery floss instead of regular thread.

Your needle and embroidery floss should be thick enough to stand out and look intentional, but shouldn't be so thick that they create permanent holes or snags in your fabric, especially if you plan to remove the stitches later. Test your chosen needle and thread in an inconspicuous spot first, and keep in mind that dye from dark floss colours can rub off onto light fabric over time and stain it.

All of these stitches were done with a double-threaded needle with a knot tied at the end.

Double thread technique:
Pull thread through needle,
tie knot at desired length.

COLOURS

Repairs that match the original fabric's colour more closely tend to read as a character wanting to keep the garment's original look intact, even if it means they may have to look harder for a thread or patch that matches. On the flip side, repairs that contrast the original fabric read as the character prioritizing functionality over aesthetics in their clothing. This can be a fun thing to explore if you want to inject some headcanon into your cosplay!

Faux Repair Stitches

There are several simple stitches that are effective to use on top of an existing seam or rip in a garment, or to attach patches. Additionally, you could even layer stitches on top of every seam on a garment to give the impression that it was originally assembled hastily with large stitches. This can be a cool detail on garments such as an outfit for a tiny character such as a fairy, or if the garment is made from a thick material such as leather or canvas.

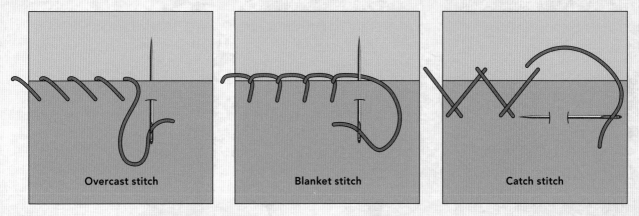

Overcast stitch   Blanket stitch   Catch stitch

Patches

Patches are a time-honoured way to show that a piece of clothing is old and tattered. They're super easy to attach and remove, so they're perfect for those basic pieces such as shirts and trousers that you plan to wear again. Square and rectangular patches are a classic shape, though triangular and round ones can also sometimes look interesting.

If your cosplay is mostly solid fabrics, this also might be a cool opportunity to add a small splash of pattern and utilize some cool scraps. You can even dirty up a patch with paint before attaching it to give it some dimension, using the techniques in Shadows, Highlights, and Dirt (page 107) as inspiration.

Darning

If patches are too basic for your taste and you want to switch things up a bit, darning an imaginary hole is a really fun (and surprisingly convincing) way to add physical breakdown.

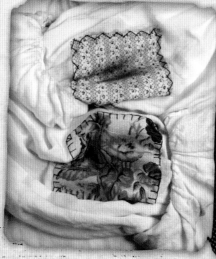

FAUX DARNING

To add faux darning, you start by drawing out where you want your "hole" to be with tailors' chalk and then create the darning weave over top of it with thread.

1. Draw your faux hole with chalk.

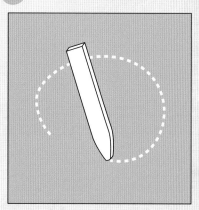

2. Stitch across the bottom of your circle, bringing your needle back up to the top of the fabric just beyond the end of your stitch.

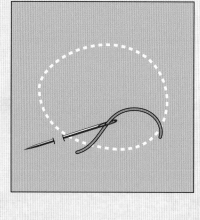

3. Stitch back across your hole in the opposite direction, just above the stitch you just made, again bringing your thread back to the top of the fabric just beyond the end of your stitch.

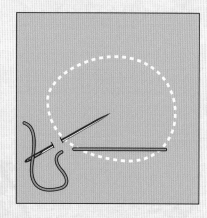

4. Repeat.

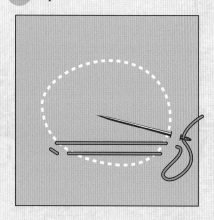

5. Continue to add stitches until you reach the top of your hole.

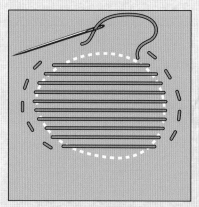

6. From the top of your hole, weave your needle down through your stitches.

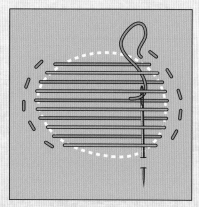

Every other stitch has been coloured orange for contrast.

7. Repeat the previous step, this time reversing which horizontal threads are above and below the new woven stitch.

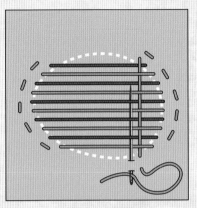

Opposite stitches have been coloured purple for contrast.

8. Continue to add woven stitches until you have covered the hole. Begin echoing the stitches around the perimeter of the darned area.

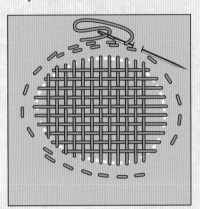

9. When you reach the opposite edge, add more woven stitches.

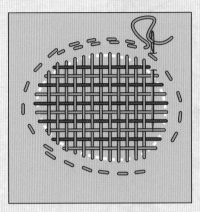

10. Finished!

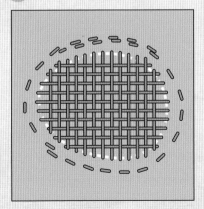

BREAKING RULES

Pulling the thread just a little bit tight on the long stitches causes the fabric to bunch up and form a small gap underneath the thread weave. While this isn't what you should do when darning something properly, the shadow that forms under the weave when you do this intentionally can actually enhance the illusion, making it look as though there really is a hole in the garment.

Mismatched Buttons

Mismatched buttons give the impression that the garment has lost a button and the character attempted to repair it themselves with varying degrees of success. This technique is super quick and easy to do.

Simply use a seam ripper to remove one or more of your buttons and replace it with a button that looks similar, but isn't exactly the same. To make sure your original button doesn't get lost, attach it with either a few temporary stitches or a safety pin to the inside of the garment. Sometimes, you can simply turn the same button backward and get a different look that way instead.

Hanging by a Thread

While not technically a fake repair, *swing tacks*—thread chains that attach materials while allowing some movement—are the perfect thing to use for making all kinds of pieces look like they're about to fall off, all while remaining perfectly secure. A swing tack can attach anything from a button or fastener to a tattered piece of cloth that you want to have a little more security.

MAKE A SWING TACK

1. Make a few stitches in the first part of the fabric you wish to join.

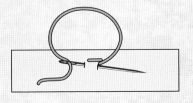

BUTTONS

You can also attach a button with a swing tack to make it look as though it's hanging off. Simply tie your starting thread through the button shank instead of making tacks in a piece of fabric and continue making the chain as normal.

2. Leave a loop and hold your thread over top of it.

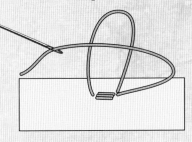

3. Pull the thread through the loop, but keep the needle on the same side.

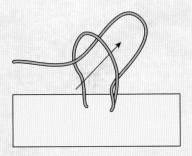

4. Pull the loop tight, creating a new loop.

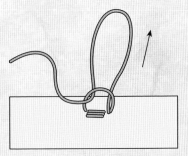

5. Repeat steps 2–4, creating a chain.

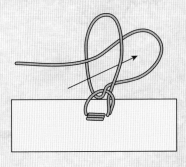

6. The length of the chain is up to you and how far you want your piece to hang, though the most stable ones tend to be 2″ (5cm) long or less.

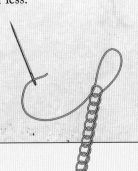

7. Pull your needle through the top loop and pull it tight.

8. Make a few anchor stitches in the other part of the fabric, connecting the two halves with the chain. Fasten off.

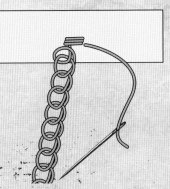

Holes, Cuts, AND RIPS

Artistically ripping apart a cosplay may seem scary at first, but it can be just as much fun to take a garment apart as it is to put one together. It becomes less about destroying something and more about elevating it into something super dramatic and exciting. The most important thing to consider is the physical cause of the rip, as holes may be different shapes or sizes depending on whether they were made by a blade, a claw, a bullet, or simply wear and tear.

Fresh-looking tears in a garment from events such as a fight are singular and distinct and are usually made by cutting with a blade, such as scissors or a knife. These fresh tears may have some fraying, but generally not as much as holes from wear over time.

If you want a hole to look as though it was made by a thicker object, such as a bullet or claw, the hole should have more stretching than fraying. You can mimic the piercing force with some sandpaper wrapped around a dowel.

Finally, holes from wear and tear are made by friction in real life, so in order to get holes that have the right look, you would create them with friction here as well, using sandpaper and rocks.

COSPLAYER: Marquise Cubey
COSTUME: Little Sister from *Bioshock 2*
Photo by John Rotor-Murphy

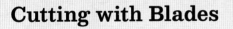

COSPLAYER: Vic Trevino
COSTUME: Vicar Amelia from *Bloodborne*
Photo by David Ngo

Cutting with Blades

If you know that you want your rips or holes in a specific place or shape, it's a good idea to start by cutting them with a blade such as a craft knife or some sharp fabric scissors.

Even though fabric tends to rip on the straight grain in real life, it often looks significantly more interesting to cut diagonal and jagged lines into your fabric, even when you're aiming for a realistic look. An effective, natural-looking way to do this is to pull sideways on the fabric as you cut into it.

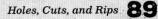

You can also cut holes into fabric. Pinch the fabric into a fold and cut it with your scissors, resulting in an easy organic shape.

To mimic the look of fabric that has been pierced by an object thicker or duller than a sharp sword or knife, first cut into the fabric with a blade. Then, roll some sandpaper into a tube or around a dowel or pencil and use it to stretch out an "exit point."

HOLEY SACRILEGE

Using holes in a weathered cosplay is a lot like using spicy peppers in a meal: They can add a ton of excitement, but they're not appropriate for every character—even otherwise heavily weathered ones— so they need to be used and placed wisely! Approach lightly at first, and ramp it up if the costume needs more. Most important, though, is making sure the placement of your holes won't compromise the garment's structure or cause wardrobe malfunctions.

Fraying

SAFETY FIRST!

Techniques for making holes, cuts, and rips can cause the release of particulate matter and must be done in a well-ventilated space with the appropriate PPE.

NON-FRAYING RIPS

If, for stylistic reasons, you don't want your holes to fray, use some clear fabric glue around the raw edges to keep them from falling apart.

A hand ruffer

Cuts with very little fraying and texture read as cartoony and stylized. This is great if you're going in that artistic direction, but when opting for a more realistic look, it is important that they have at least a little bit of fraying, stretching, and pulling to convey some cause and effect.

The easiest way to fray something is by using any tool with a lot of sharp pointy bits to pull at threads along the raw edges. The most accessible of these tools are fine graters, such as the type meant for hard cheeses, and wire cleaning brushes. If you're fancy, though, you can also use a leatherworking tool called a *hand ruffer*. While much more expensive, these specialized tools are particularly powerful and versatile weathering tools because their hooked spikes can grab and pull loose threads far more easily than a wire brush can. This makes it a great tool to use when you're trying to sell a bit of weathering as a slash from a blunt item, such as a bullet or a claw.

A wire-cleaning brush from the dollar store being used to pull at threads on a hem.

DEFYING GRAVITY

If the laws of physics are keeping you from getting the dramatic tears of your dreams, you can swing tack certain parts together with matching thread to help your garment keep its shape, as well as make it more structurally sound than it looks. For a refresher on making swing tacks, turn to Hanging by a Thread (page 86).

This rip is maybe a bit too gravity defying.

Adding a swing tack

Securely and all-but-invisibly attached!

Textured Holes

Textured holes are great for implying that a garment has been worn down by friction or the elements over a long period of time. Large holes read as being made by wear, such as a large hole in a knee or elbow. Soft smaller holes, on the other hand, give the look of fabric that is gradually being eaten away by the elements.

Fabric before adding this additional layer of texture

With textured holes

Rough rocks are a surprisingly useful tool for creating this effect.

Place a rough rock behind your fabric and sand across the top with sandpaper to create a bunch of soft, textural holes. Differently shaped parts of a rock can also be used to create holes of different sizes and textures, so it's great to experiment.

Another more controlled way to create textured holes is to use a seam ripper to rip a very small hole in your fabric.

Sand it lightly with sandpaper to soften up the edges.

Seam rippers can also be used to create small holes in the top layer of interfaced pieces, such as collars and cuffs.

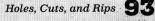

COSPLAYER: Jessilyn Cupcake
COSTUME: Mad Moxxi from *Borderlands 2*
Photo by Jessilyn Cupcake

PART 4

THE FREEDOM OF PAINTING

Fabric Painting 101

Fabric painting is a lot more like regular painting than one might think, but it does differ in some important ways. This chapter covers some crucial things to keep in mind so that your fabric painting can look as close to your vision as possible.

Painting Fabric

Acrylic paint is inexpensive, versatile, and comes in every colour under the sun. Contrary to popular belief, it is absolutely possible to use it on fabric in a way that has very little effect on the texture and drape.

The key to achieving this is to strive to use as little acrylic paint as possible. This goes for both dry-brushed techniques and for techniques using watered-down paint. If you find that you must use more paint in order to get more solid coverage, consider switching to fabric paint, fabric ink, or even dye, as these will remain soft and flexible when dry.

Layering

You're already familiar with the larger-scale weathering covered in The Layered Process of Weathering (page 26), but did you know that you can also use layering in your individual painted effects? No matter what you're painting, it is great to have at least one darker colour and one lighter colour for each effect. Start out by using the darker colour, and then when you're finished, layer on one or two lighter colours in the middle to create highlights.

THERE ARE NO MISTAKES, ONLY HAPPY ACCIDENTS

With weathering, it's always important to be intentional about every splatter and cut so that they look like they were part of your artistic vision and not a mistake. That being said, if you do make a mistake when weathering, see if you can roll with it and add some backstory to explain the mistake. You can do this by painting accidental stains to be bigger and more obvious, or you could even try replicating that oopsie somewhere else on the garment.

Painting Pleather and Leather

Even if you aren't weathering the rest of your cosplay, the difference between a lightly weathered leather, pleather, or vinyl accessory and a clean one is night and day, especially if you're trying to pass off synthetic leather as genuine.

ACCESSORY: Tiny Tina shoes from *Borderlands 2*
Photo by Jessilyn Cupcake

Paints

While most of these weathering techniques for painting can be used as written on many fabrics, it's important to note that regular acrylic paint doesn't stick very well to leather or pleather. When you are painting on shadows, make sure that you're using flexible paints meant for leather. To pick a paint, turn to Types of Paint (page 103)!

However, the fact that regular paint doesn't stick can be used in creative ways. For example, while the shadows on this white belt were done with leather paint, the stitching was painted with watered-down acrylic paint and then quickly wiped away with a paper towel, leaving behind just the painted thread.

LEATHER REFERENCES

When you're looking for references for aged leather and pleather, some of the best things you can look at are shoes, even if you aren't necessarily weathering a pair of them. Using one of your own shoes as a reference is even better because it's a real object that you can hold up right next to your costume piece in the same lighting.

Finishing and Storing a Painted Cosplay

The final step in painting a costume is to heat-set your hard work by blasting it with hot air for 15 minutes. This step is crucial, as it minimizes the risk of your paint rubbing off on other things.

You can use any machine dryer to heat-set your clothes once the paint has dried completely. If you don't have easy access to a machine dryer, or if you've painted something like shoes and tossing them into a machine may ruin them, you can also place the garments or items inside a zipped garment bag and stick the nose of a hair dryer in through the hole where the hanger would usually poke out.

SAFETY FIRST!
Make sure to keep the hair dryer's heat on low so that it doesn't burn or melt your garment bag, and never leave it unattended while it's running.

Storage

The best way to store weathered cosplays is by hanging them up on hangers. Even if you've heat-set your costume, you should still treat each item as though the paint has the potential to rub off onto other things, especially if you end up travelling with your costumes in a suitcase. For this, a garment bag is once again your best friend.

Use the garment bag over the hanger as you normally would when hanging your costume in the closet. When you're travelling, place the costume inside the bag before folding it up and packing it. This way, the bag not only protects it and your other belongings, but it protects the costume from itself too, making sure paint doesn't rub off onto parts of the garment that shouldn't have paint.

Brushes and Painting
TOOLS

There are dozens of different brushes, paints, and other tools in any given art store, and they're all great for different jobs. Here are a bunch of cool brushes that I've found to be the best to have on hand when painting and weathering textiles for cosplay; paints and more specific tools are covered in their respective chapters.

Paintbrushes

The cool thing about painting fabric for weathering is you actually don't need tons of expensive brushes or tools, especially since painting fabric can be quite rough on your nice brushes. It is, however, often better to use brushes with natural bristles for realistic weathering rather than ones with synthetic bristles, especially when you're watering down paint. Natural bristles are porous and absorb the paint, making it easier to work with; plus, unlike the times where you're painting something solid and smooth, the natural unevenness of a natural brush can add a lot of character when weathering.

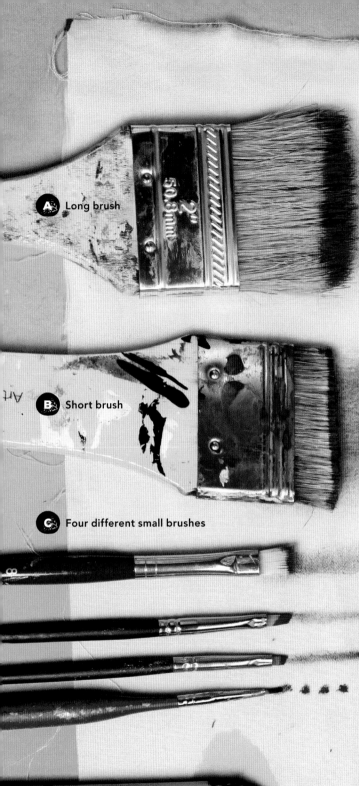

A Long brush

B Short brush

C Four different small brushes

D Squirrel calligraphy brush

A *Long Brushes*

Cheap paintbrushes with rough natural bristles are my absolute favourite things to use for natural-looking weathering, and they're awesome for light, feathery dry brushing and watered-down paint.

B *Short Brushes*

Painting fabric with more heavy-looking dry brushing can be a pain in the butt due to all the friction, so rough brushes with short, cut-off bristles make it easier to drive paint into fabric. The best part about rough paintbrushes being super cheap is that you can buy a few of them, cut the bristles down on some until they're short and solid, and leave others as they are for lighter work.

C *Small Brushes*

Small brushes are used for detail work and stylized weathering. Small brushes with shorter bristles can be used to paint shadows onto seams to help them pop more in photos, which is great on colours that are difficult to photograph such as red or white.

D *Ink and Calligraphy Brushes*

These are great for fabric inks and even fibre-reactive dyes (page 46) since they soak them right up and don't drip as much. However, they are delicate and aren't ideal for acrylics and heavier paints.

KEEPING YOUR BRUSHES CLEAN

Remember to wash your brushes with soap and warm water after every crafting session to help them last longer. Hand sanitizer also breaks down acrylic paint, and it can be used in a pinch to rescue hardened brushes.

Spray bottle with water

Spray paint can

Stencil sponge

Sponges

Stencil brushes

Airbrush

Stencil

Other Painting Tools

Sponges

You can find both synthetic and natural sponges and sponge brushes in art and craft stores. Natural sponges in particular are awesome for creating organic-looking textures far more easily than with paintbrushes and work particularly well with watered-down paint.

Spray Bottle and Water

Spraying down your fabric before painting is essential to creating a permanent "wet look" that looks convincing even when the fabric is dry. These tools are also really handy to have on hand for watering down paint.

Stencil Brushes and Sponges

The bristles on a stencil brush are blunt and flat. While they may not be ideal for dragging paint across a fabric, they are perfect for the vertical, light stabbing motion used in stencilling. Stencil sponges are the exact same, just with a sponge instead of a brush.

Spray Cans

While spray paint doesn't leave you with the softest fabric when it dries, it's hard to dismiss it completely because it will always be super fast and convenient for large, even-looking spots, such as the look of soot all over clothing. Make sure to only use these paints outside and to wear a mask and disposable gloves, as the fumes will make you sick.

Airbrushes

Airbrushes give you the fast, uniform, brush stroke–free application of spray paint, combined with the power to mix your own colours. That being said, airbrushes can also be expensive and fiddly, so while they're fantastic for things such as clean shadows and stencils if you happen to own one already, they are not necessary for every cosplayer's needs.

Paints, Inks, and
PIGMENTS

The world of paint is a vast and exciting one, and there are different types for different projects. Here's a guide to finding the best paint for your needs.

Types of Paint

These are the most common kinds of paints that you will come across for painting and weathering fabric.

Acrylic Paint

Easy to find, affordable, and super versatile, acrylics can even be mixed with different mediums to give them texture and to make them suitable for fabric and airbrushing.

Flexible Paint

These paints are great at sticking to shoes, leather, armour, and anything else that takes a lot of physical stress—without cracking. Some common brands are PlaidFX and Angelus Leather Paint.

Fabric Paint

Fabric paint, as you may have guessed, is great for fabric. It bonds to fabric more easily, and as long as it's driven really well into the fabric, it will hold up to stretching and washing while staying softer and more flexible than regular acrylic paint. It's ideal for solid, unbroken patches of colour.

Puffy Fabric Paint

It's fabric paint, but it stays three-dimensional when it dries! You can even blast it with a heat gun (while wearing a vapour respirator, of course) to create interesting bubbly textures.

Fabric Ink

Fabric ink is similar to fabric paint, except it's even softer and thinner. It can be ideal for detail work as well as block and screen printing, stencilling, and anything else where less texture is desired.

SPACERS

Paint often bleeds through to the other side or layers of a piece of clothing. In order to avoid this, make sure to put a spacer such as a piece of cardboard or plastic between garment layers or hold the garment open with your arm. If you own a dress form, you can cover it with a plastic garbage bag and put the garment over the top so you can paint on a human-shaped form.

Nail Polish

Nail polish is great for easily painting plastic or metallic buttons and fasteners since it's made to bond easily to hard, smooth surfaces. Just don't make the same mistake I did and use it on something that has already been painted with acrylic paint, because boy, it sure does dissolve acrylic paint!

Temporary Pigments

It's common for cosplayers to incorporate basic pieces such as pants and shoes into their costumes to save money and time, but if your cosplay involves a lot of heavy breakdown and weathering, you may not want clean pants or shiny black shoes to throw off your carefully crafted vision. Luckily, you can use all kinds of temporary pigments to add character without the commitment that comes with regular paint.

Temporary Pigments

Cocoa powder is good for replicating the look of dirt, and you probably already have some in your kitchen.

Flour or cornstarch can be used on their own to create a faded look or mixed with other kitchen ingredients to make their colours lighter.

Cinnamon has a reddish colour that makes it ideal to mix with cocoa powder if you want a little colour variation for dirt effects.

Schmere Pigment Powder is the go-to fake dirt used by pros in the entertainment industry. The big benefit of using Schmere powder rather than kitchen ingredients is that you have access to more natural-looking dirt colours, especially ones that are slightly more grey or green. It comes in either a powder form or a stick form like a big crayon that lets you draw directly onto the garment.

MATERIAL SOURCES

Schmere powder can be found online at most film and theatrical costume supply stores; check out the Resources section (page 126).

Eyeshadow can be comparatively expensive for the small amount you get, but it's more accessible than professional pigments and a great way to use up an expired palette you already own. It can also be useful for more fantasy-inspired weathering colours that aren't available in typical pigment lineups.

Applying Temporary Pigments

All of these pigments, aside from Schmere Ageing Crayons, are powders. This means they aren't as stable as traditional paint and may rub off on things if they are applied like powdered makeup.

To help these powders both stick to the garment and wash out more easily, apply a clear, washable primer to your fabric before painting them on. These primers can include things like petroleum jelly or a light coat of hairspray. Make sure to apply hairspray lightly, as too much can make your fabric stiff.

If you're not a fan of the powdery look, you can also mix your pigment powders with a washable medium. Mixing the powder with water will give you a soft, subtle look similar to watered-down paint, and mixing with hair-spray will give you a darker, richer colour with more clumps. Mineral or baby oil mixed with pigments will give you a neat soaked-in look, but it can take a little more effort to wash out.

IT'S TEMPORARY, BUT IS IT WASHABLE?

Before using any of these pigments, primers, or mediums, do a few tests on a scrap or an inconspicuous part of the garment, wait until it dries completely, and see if you are able to wash it out without the pigment staining the garment.

Shadows, Highlights,  AND DIRT

Painting isn't just great for weathered cosplays, it's also great for bringing to life certain anime, comic, and video game–based costumes and for emphasizing construction details on regular, "clean" costumes. This is especially true if your fabric is difficult to photograph and you have cool-looking seams that you want to show off.

SOMETHING OTHER THAN BROWN

If the media you're cosplaying has an iconic colour palette for its environments and lighting, it can be fun to mix hints of those bright colours into your shading and dirt palette. Even if it doesn't make logical sense, it can be a super cool way to sneak in some individuality and subtle homage.

COSPLAYER: Marquise Cubey
COSTUME: Protagonist from *Persona 3*
Photo by John Rotor-Murphy

Some phthalo green was mixed into the shadow colour used on my white gun belt for the Persona 3 protagonist, giving it a hint of surreal colour that also complemented the red details on the uniform.

Realistic Shading and Dirt

The best way to achieve many costume weathering effects is by *dry brushing* them on, using a short-bristled brush to drive in bolder colours and a long-bristled one for a lighter, wispy look. As the name implies, your paintbrush should have as little paint loaded onto it as possible, to the point that it's practically dry!

Shadows

Use a small, short brush to dry brush shadows and dust onto seams. As a general rule, your seam shadows should be no wider than ¼″ (0.5cm). If you do wish to break this rule and make them wider, it can make your costume look ultra dirty, so make sure first that's the look you want.

Make sure to get underneath overlapping pieces as well for a full effect, using a larger brush or an airbrush.

If you are painting something, such as this gun holster, and you know that part of the piece will always be facing the ground, you can dry brush larger shadows on those undersides.

COSPLAYER: Marquise Cubey
COSTUME: Gina Lestrade from *The Great Ace Attorney*
Photo by John Rotor-Murphy

POCKETS, HOLSTERS, AND SCABBARDS

If you are weathering a pocket that you know will have a specific prop inside it, paint it with either the prop or a similarly shaped object in the pocket so you can reflect its shape with your shading. If you're worried about the prop getting paint on it, wrap it in a plastic bag to protect it.

Dirt

When painting dirt onto your costume, start with the logical places for dirt to appear. These include areas near hems, on elbows and knees, and around existing physical wear. You can even add dirt effects to enhance battle damage.

Once you've applied dirt effects to all of those places, add some extra spots here and there for asymmetry.

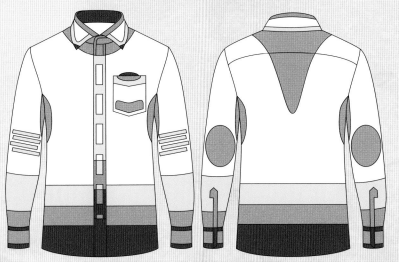

Additional areas for added dirt on shirts

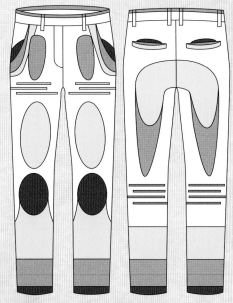

Additional areas for added dirt on pants

Ageing Fasteners, Buttons, and Hardware

If you've spent lots of time painting shadows and breakdown onto a costume but the shiny metallic fasteners are throwing off your aesthetic, all you need is some black nail polish and disposable gloves to tone them down.

Simply add a few dabs of black nail polish onto your hardware and rub it all over with your fingers, taking care to not get nail polish on the surrounding area. To help the polish adhere better, you can also sand the metallic surfaces with fine-grit sandpaper before painting.

Stylized Shading and Highlights

Realistic shadows are soft and subtle, but if you desire a cel-shaded effect that looks like it came straight from a cartoon, you should make your shadows look as solid as possible. It's essential to note, however, that solid colours painted with acrylic paint will turn hard and brittle when they dry on fabric, so in order for your costume to retain its drape, you'd want to use fabric ink, fabric paint, or flexible paint.

For a comic book dot-shading and cross-hatching effect, use stencils to keep the texture uniform. To apply the paint, use a stencil brush in a stabbing motion.

HEIGHTENED REALITY

While the majority of the texture in a cartoony, stylized costume is painted on and clearly not real, in order for it to be effective, lines and wrinkles should still be in believable places.

COSPLAYER: Jessilyn Cupcake
COSTUME: Tiny Tina from *Borderlands 3*
Photo by Jessilyn Cupcake

Wet Stains and
SPLATTERS

We've covered many types of weathering for emulating shadows to dirt, but what about the kind of weathering you'd use to imply damp conditions? This chapter is all about the different ways you can use watered-down paints, pigments, and, sometimes, fibre-reactive dyes (page 46).

As you may imagine, significantly watering down your paint will give a different appearance than dry brushing—a soft, watercolour-like look. A spray bottle filled with water is not only an excellent tool to have on hand for spraying down your garment before painting but is also an easily accessible source of water to spray onto your paint palette a little at a time.

COSPLAYER: Marquise Cubey
COSTUME: Little Sister from *Bioshock 2*
Photo by John Rotor-Murphy

Lighter Stains

Watered-down paint is best used for lighter, translucent stains. It works great with all of the brushes you'd use for dry brushing and works especially well when applied with natural sponges to larger areas.

If you want your stain to be seeped-in and soft, spray your fabric with water before painting it.

If you want your stain to have a hard edge, paint directly onto the dry fabric with watered-down paint.

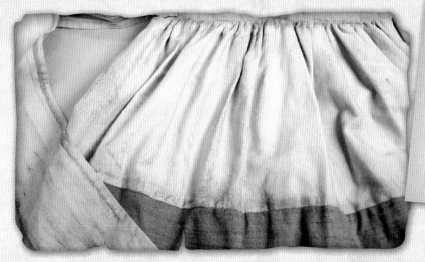

If you want to give something a permanently wet look, first spray the area that you wish to paint with water. Mix your paint colour as close as you can get to the colour of the wet material. Then, mix in some "dirt" colours such as raw and burnt umber to help the colour stand out more!

Use a short brush to paint onto seams and along hems and other edges. As you normally would, start out light first and see how things look. If you feel like your stains could use some more visual interest, try painting your stains larger or darker toward the bottom edges to simulate the pull of gravity.

GOING GREEN

A warm green paint that you would normally use to imply organic matter such as grass stains can also be mixed into your paint to give the impression of algae or sewer water. The mix to the left used chromium oxide green.

Darker Stains

For large, dark sections of colour, you may want to start off by dyeing your garment. In this example, I started out by doing a red dip-dye on the bottom half of the skirt. If you need a refresher on how to do this, check out Dip-Dyeing (page 69).

If, after dip-dyeing something, you decide that you need more colour or a deeper colour, you can go over the parts that you would like to be darker, such as the edges, with watered-down paint.

For a convincing look, you can use the wet-look technique, mixing the paint to match the wet fabric after spraying it with water.

Splats

To create a splatter, load any paintbrush with watered-down paint or fabric ink. If your splatter should look like something opaque like oil or even fake blood, you only need just enough water to get the paint to a runny consistency.

While wearing disposable gloves, flick the bristles with your fingers, moving your hand in the opposite direction to the splatter. Different-sized paintbrushes create different-sized splatters.

Experiment with your own collection of brushes and see which ones you prefer.

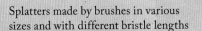

Splatters made by brushes in various sizes and with different bristle lengths

Extreme Weathering and
FAKE BLOOD

A book about weathering that doesn't go into detail about horror-based effects would be like a hoedown with no music—missing exactly what you came to see!

Even though this chapter references techniques from previous chapters, effects like burns, decay, and blood all have more specific colours and textures associated with them. These extreme effects are the culmination of texture, technique, and colour crashing together, and they are insanely fun to create.

Puff Paint 3D Texture

Puffy fabric paint is a secret weapon of sorts among entertainment industry breakdown artists and ager/dyers. If you have a respirator mask on hand, you can use puff paint to create some really cool-looking crumbly textures that are great for imitating things like mould, ash, and more, depending on the colours you use.

SAFETY FIRST!

This technique involves both the release of particulate matter as well as harmful vapours, and it must be done in a well-ventilated space with the appropriate PPE.

CREATING 3D TEXTURE

MATERIALS	TOOLS AND EQUIPMENT	
Garment	Vapour respirator	Heat-resistant work gloves
Puffy fabric paint	Dust mask	Rough paintbrushes
	Safety goggles	Heat gun

Process

1. Dry brush an initial layer of puffy fabric paint onto your fabric.

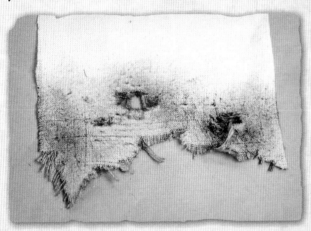

2. Use the puffy fabric paint again to paint a second heavier, 3D layer. If the garment you're painting is torn or shredded, try to make this second layer connect all of the edges and holes, giving the illusion that the garment is being eaten away by mould or flames.

3. While working outside or in a ventilated garage and wearing a respirator mask with vapour cartridges installed, use your heat gun to blow hot air at the puff paint. The paint should expand, crumble, and crack, creating a 3D texture.

4. If you want to emphasize the texture, you can lightly dry brush over the puffs with another colour to give it some highlights.

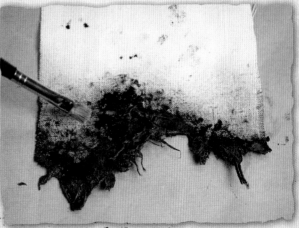

Burns and Ash

Sometimes, you can set a costume on fire to make it look as though it's been burned, but fire can be unpredictable and afterward, you're often left with ash that can rub off onto other things. Instead, it may be a better idea to paint burns using our layered approach.

Physical Holes

Before you paint your fabric, the first thing you should do is to tear it up using the techniques in Holes, Cuts, and Rips (page 88), removing some of the material as a fire would. If you have a realistic look in mind, edges softened using sandpaper and rocks will read as a more believable texture for burns, whereas harder edges will look more stylized.

2D Painting

If you're adding a large amount of black ash to a piece of clothing such as the bottom of a coat, simply dry brushing, airbrushing, or even lightly spray painting your ash on usually works well. Layering still looks great no matter what, though, so try using a mix of black toward the middle and lighter grey on the edges.

3D Painting

If you want your ash to look bubbly and realistic, use the Puff Paint 3D Texture method (page 116) with black puff paint, then dry brush a lighter grey on top.

GLOWING EMBERS

If you want to look as though you are still slightly on fire, use a very small detail brush to paint tiny orange and gold flecks onto every other frayed thread. Metallic gold paint in particular will reflect light and give off more of a "glow."

Mould and Extreme Decay

A touch of mould is a great way to add a bit of colour and visual interest to an undead character's clothes. For something dead and rotting, you want the look of fungus rather than flora, so bright, bluish greens such as phthalo green mixed with a bit of a warm black such as mars black around the edges with white highlights will instantly read as gross mould.

Easy Mould

Start off by sanding some small textural holes with the rock method in Holes, Cuts, and Rips (page 88) in random places on the garment, and then use the appropriate colours with techniques in either Shadows, Highlights, and Dirt (page 107) or Wet Stains and Splatters (page 112) to easily achieve a basic mouldy look.

Doing Research to Push Your Effects Further

When it comes to clothes that are decaying and breaking apart, all kinds of interesting effects, colours, and textures can happen unpredictably, so it's also extremely useful to look at the real thing.

Now that you know how to go about achieving many kinds of textures on fabric, try looking for a cool-looking piece of real decayed clothing on the internet and see if you can break down the specific things you'd do to replicate it. Would you dip-dye it with a resist? Would you tear it up? Would you maybe even create 3D clusters using puff paint? The possibilities are infinite, and breaking down a small effect like this can end up being just as fun as breaking down the process for an entire costume.

SEARCH KEYWORDS

When looking for reference pictures of dilapidated clothes on the internet, "clothes decay" is a much more useful term to start off your search than "clothes decomposing." The former search term contains all kinds of well-lit art exhibits, while the latter contains more photos of landfills and, if you're unlucky, other things decomposing along with the clothes that you may not have asked to see!

COSPLAYER: Lutavia Cosplay
COSTUME: Bela Dimitrescu from *Resident Evil Village*
Photo by Yinyue Photography

Fake Blood

Blood is super interesting, and it can be a noticeably different colour depending on the severity of the injury, the part of the body it's from, how long it's been exposed to the air, and more.

Arterial: Bright and Screaming

Your arteries are located deeper below your skin and bleed faster than veins, so the bright red blood from them is associated with very serious injuries. People also simply have stronger emotional reactions to brighter reds, making it super striking.

Your paint for arterial red blood should have the slightest hint of blue mixed into it, as it can veer into spaghetti sauce territory pretty quickly if you just use red by itself.

Venous: Dark and Foreboding

Veins are usually located closer to the surface of your skin than arteries, so the darker blood that comes from them is associated with less life-threatening injuries like cuts and scratches. Despite this, however, the fact that it shows up in everyday injuries makes it instantly recognizable as realistic blood, and that can make dark blood quite effective and scary in its own way.

For a venous look, mix more dark blue into your red than you would use for arterial blood. It's important to note that super dark venous blood won't show up as well on dark fabric or dark skin sometimes, so make sure the colour is bright enough to still pop.

Dried Blood

Both arterial and venous blood dry to a similar dull, rusty colour, and dry bloodstains can be a fun way to give a sense of history to your character, such as a reference to a horror villain's previous victims.

Since the rusty colour comes from the iron in blood, red oxide is the best colour to use as a base because it uses real iron oxide as a pigment. Adding a hint of blue will help it read more as blood, a brighter red can be added to help it stand out more against a dark background, and raw umber can be mixed in if you wish to darken it.

VISUAL RESEARCH FOR BLOOD

While studying the real-life effects you're trying to replicate is usually best, if you're a hobbyist who is recreating a specific type of wound, you're often better off using artistic recreations as visual references instead of the real thing. If the recreation looks at all convincing, nine times out of ten this is because the artist that made it has already done the dirty research work of studying real wounds and corpses. As such, their recreations are often detailed perfectly well enough for you to use as a visual guide.

Permanent Blood

If you are planning to travel with your cosplay or store it with fake blood on it, you will generally want to paint it on so that it ends up being dry to the touch and doesn't get all over everything else. Since blood stains are meant to read as "liquid," they can be done with slightly watered-down paint or fabric ink. Blood is also relatively opaque and thick, so you should only add as much water as you need to get the paint to a runny consistency.

Temporary Blood

Some store-bought fake blood for stage use can be washed out of clothing, but not all of it is created equally. As with any temporary weathering pigment, make sure to test it on a scrap piece of fabric of a similar colour and fibre content. You need to see if it washes out before you use it on your real costume piece even if you've used it on a different fabric in the past.

Children's washable paint is another way to get fake blood effects that can, theoretically, wash out and are also dry to the touch. Just make sure to skip the step of heat-setting your paint. With a bit of effort, this paint can wash out of many fabrics.

Finally, a great way to get fake blood that looks fresh and shiny but is also dry to the touch and washable is by using cheap brushes to apply melted children's washable crayons as though they were paint. You can even break the crayons into pieces and mix different colours with each other before melting them if you want to adjust the colour.

Final Word:
PUTTING IT ALL TOGETHER

Now that you know all of these cool techniques, you can expand your horizons and adapt them to other types of effects and maybe even discover new ways to create them that works best for your style.

There's a whole world of specific effects that I haven't even covered, but I hope that I helped you become better at searching for them and coming up with brand-new ones. Keep in mind, I'm only scratching the surface of what you can do with paint and cosplay!

Recommended Reading

If you enjoyed this book and want to learn even more about the world of costumes, weathering, and textile arts, these are some incredible books that are totally worth checking out.

Fabric Painting and Dyeing for the Theatre
by Deborah M. Dryden

The Costume Technician's Handbook
by Rosemary Ingham and Liz Covey

Advanced Cosplay Painting—Airbrush and Weathering
by Svetlana Quindt and Benjamin Schwarz

Painting and Weathering for Props and Replicas
by Harrison Krix

Painting on Fabric by Naraku Brock

APPENDICES

Appendix A: Dye Test Results Template

Weight of fibre	Colour(s) used and ratio	Depth of shade (%)	Salt added (mL)	Vinegar added (mL)	Time	Water temp.	Finished sample (attached)

Appendix B: Metric Conversion Chart

Teaspoons	Tablespoons	Cups	Fluid Ounces	Milliliter
1				4.93
2				9.86
3	1	1/16	1/2	14.79
4				19.72
5				24.64
6	2	1/8	1	29.57
7				34.50
8				39.43
9	3	3/16	1½	44.36
10				49.29
11				54.22
12	4	¼	2	59.15
	5	5/16	2½	73.93
	6	3/8	3	88.72
	7	7/16	3½	103.51
	8	½	4	118.29
	9	9/16	4½	133.08
	10	5/8	5	147.87
	11	11/16	5½	162.65
	12	¾	6	177.44
	13	13/16	6½	192.23
	14	7/8	7	207.02
	15	15/16	7½	221.80
	16	1	8	236.59

RESOURCES

Textile Art and Dye Suppliers

Dharma Trading Co. (United States) dharmatrading.com

Maiwa Handprints (Canada) maiwa.com

George Weil (United Kingdom) georgeweil.com

patchworkshop.de (Germany/EU) patchworkshop.de

Entertainment Industry Costume and Makeup Suppliers

Manhattan Wardrobe Supply (United States) wardrobesupplies.com

HollyNorth (Canada) hollynorth.com

TILT Professional Makeup (United Kingdom) tiltmakeup.com

PATIN-A (Germany/EU) patin-a.de/en

About the
AUTHOR

Julianna Franchini (also known by her online alias, MarquiseCubey) was born and raised near the rocky shores of Vancouver, British Columbia, and has been sewing for as long as she can remember. She started out as a kid, making clothes for her dolls and eventually herself, and discovered the world of cosplay as a teen. She was inspired to continue with a formal education in costuming for film and theatre, which helped infuse her cosplays with a tangible expression of her love of garment history and storytelling. When she's not making or wearing costumes, Julianna is playing bass guitar, hanging out with her budgie, discussing the complex inner lives of video game characters, and sharing her knowledge and love of costuming with fellow cosplayers in the community.

VISIT JULIANNA ONLINE AND FOLLOW ON SOCIAL MEDIA!

Website: marquisecubey.com

Twitter: @marquisecubey

Instagram: @marquisecubey

TikTok: @marquisecubey

FanPowered
PRESS

Developed with our cosplay authors, FanPowered Press evokes how C&T's authors inspire and expand crafting topics by presenting innovative methods and ideas. We hope to inspire you to jump into something new and get outside of your comfort zone!

Want more creative content? Visit us online at **ctpub.com**